The Official Rules

Books by Paul Dickson

Think Tanks

The Great American Ice Cream Book

The Future of the Workplace

The Electronic Battlefield

The Mature Person's Guide to Kites, Yo-Yos, Frisbees and Other
Childlike Diversions

Out of This World: American Space Photography

The Future File

Chow: A Cook's Tour of Military Food

The Official Rules

Paul Dickson

THE OFFICIAL RULES

Illustrated by Kenneth Tiews

•

A DELTA SPECIAL

To Andrew and Alexander—may they figure out the rules
quicker than their old man—and to the late H. Allen Smith, a hero
of mine who I would like to think
would have enjoyed all of this.

A DELTA BOOK
Published by
Dell Publishing Co., Inc.
1 Dag Hammarskjold Plaza
New York, New York 10017

Delta ® TM 755118, Dell Publishing Co., Inc.

ISBN: 0-440-56684-3
Reprinted by arrangement with Delacorte Press

Printed in the United States of America

Second printing—November 1979

Designed by Giorgetta Bell McRee

ACKNOWLEDGMENTS

"Three Laws of Robotics" by Isaac Asimov: Used by permission of the author.

Berkeley's Laws: Reprinted with permission from "The Notebook on Common
Sense, Elementary and Advanced" copyright 1978 by and published by Berkeley
Enterprises, Inc., 815 Washington Street, Newtonville, Mass. 02160.

Preface

All things are subject to fixed laws.
 —Marcus Manilius, *Astronomica,* I, c. 40 B.C.

Natural laws have no pity.
 —Long's 22nd Note, from Robert A. Heinlein's *Time Enough for Love*

For centuries mathematics and the pure sciences held a seemingly unbreakable monopoly on natural laws, principles, and named effects. At the gradual pace of a law at a time, researchers and scholars worked to show us that some element of the universe was working in perfect accord with an immutable rule that could be stated without taking a breath.

The *Second Law of Thermodynamics,* for instance, told us that in every energy transaction some of the original energy is changed into heat energy, while *Boyle's Law* informed us that at a constant temperature the volume of a given quantity of gas is inversely proportional to the pressure on the gas. Hundreds and hundreds of laws were created, with most of the great names in science in possessive possession of at least one solid law (e.g., Newton's, Ohm's, Darwin's, Mendel's, Archimedes', Einstein's, and so forth). To get through four years of college (let alone four years of Sunday crossword puzzles) one is forced into contact with a few score such laws, which are liable to range from the *Law of Action and Reaction* to the *Laws of Vibrating Strings.* *

---

*The *Law of Action and Reaction* is the one that says for every action there is an equal and opposite reaction. The *Laws of Vibrating Strings* go like this: (1) The frequency of vibration of a wire is inversely proportional to its length. The shorter the string, the higher the pitch. (2) The frequency of vibration varies directly as the square root of tension. (3) The frequency of a vibrating string varies inversely with the square root of its weight per

Yet as new laws were discovered, posted, and accepted by the textbook publishers, people outside the hard sciences increasingly felt that a whopping injustice was in force. Not only were the soft sciences, humanities, and workaday pursuits excluded from the business of lawmaking but—even more to the point—there was a deep and demonstrable prejudice at work as all these big-name scientists were busy describing a perfect Universe when, as everyone else (including not-so-big scientists) was fully aware, it is not all that perfect.

Over the years, there were a few exceptions. Economists were able to gain acceptance for such items as the *Law of Supply and Demand* and *Say's Law* (i.e., "Supply creates its own demand"). But these were exceptions to the rule. Then in the years after World War II, more and more people began hearing series of laws—more often said than written—attached to such names as Murphy, Finagle, and Sod, which had an uncanny ability to describe things as they could be and often were—screwed up. Murphy looked right into our lives and concluded, "If anything can go wrong, it will," and Finagle was able to perceive via his *Fourth Law,* "No matter what occurs, there is always someone who believes it happened according to his pet theory." It cannot be proven, but it has been suggested that Murphy, Finagle, and their disciples (all to be discussed in the pages ahead) have helped more people get through crises, deadlines, bad days, the final phases of projects, and attacks by inanimate objects than either pep talks, uplifting epigrams, or the invocation of traditional rules. It is true that if your paperboy throws your paper in the bushes for five straight days, it can be explained by *Newton's Law of Gravity.* But it takes Murphy to explain why it is happening to *you.*

As these explanations of the perversity of nature grew in popularity and importance, other laws and principles came along to

unit of length. Thick, heavy strings vibrate more slowly and hence give tones of lower pitch.

explain how other things worked. In 1955 an obscure historian named C. Northcote Parkinson wrote an article called "Parkinson's Law," in which he showed that "Work expands so as to fill the time available for its completion." Parkinson became famous, and his law has become a permanent tenet of organizational life. Parkinson begat more laws as others brought out their own discoveries. Some were highly successful, such as Dr. Laurence J. Peter and his famous *Peter Principle* (1969), while others created laws that only those in a specific circle could fully appreciate, like the great body of laws created by and for computer programmers. By the early 1970s laws were coming in from all over and showing up everywhere: newspaper columns, books, laboratory walls. . . . What more and more people were discovering in their own lives and jobs are those universal truths which have been begging to be stated scientifically and shared with the rest of the world. In most cases these laws are being discovered by average, not famous men and women —although nothing prevents senators, scientists, press pundits, and other VIPs from getting into the act. Yet, regardless of whether a law is discovered by a Nobel laureate or an insurance company clerk, a good law is a good law and able to move around the country with remarkable speed. Unfortunately, a law often moves so quickly that it is soon separated from the person who discovered and named it. As a result an important new law like *Anthony's Law of Force* (which says, "Don't force it, get a larger hammer") is known far and wide to people who have no idea who Anthony is.

Often a group of a dozen or so new laws are collected and typed out on a sheet of paper. These sheets are drawn to copying machines like metal filings to a magnet, and once copied are posted on bulletin boards, passed out at water coolers, dropped into inter-office mail systems, and swapped at conventions. Whether by jet, teletype, or mail, a list compiled and copied in Boston on a Monday is liable to show up in Santa Monica by the end of the week. The creation and distribution of laws has become full-fledged a cultural phenomenon: a computer-age folk idiom.

What follows is the work of a person who, with the help of many, has been collecting laws in a filing box which (in mock academic style) has been dubbed the Murphy Center for the Codification of Human and Organizational Law. (More on the Murphy Center appears in the "Report from the Center" at the end of the book.)

This collection of new laws is arranged alphabetically, contains special sections on areas of special importance, and is followed by a subject index. To the extent possible each law is accompanied by the identity of the person who discovered it and, when applicable, the person who first collected it. Laws that could not be connected to their discoverers are noted with a *U*, which means "unknown to this collector." There are a number of *U*s, but this is to be expected because the nature of lawgiving is such that a good law is often separated from its owner. More confusing, words taken from the utterings of famous people have been stated as laws and named in their honor. (Conversely, famous people have been known to make up laws and affix bogus names to them. John Kenneth Galbraith has done this on several occasions. See, for instance, *Grump's Law*.) As a result of this, one is liable to come up with a law like *Parker's Law of Parliamentary Procedure* ("A motion to adjourn is always in order") and have no way of knowing if the Parker in question was (a) Dorothy Parker, (b) Charlie Parker, (c) a claims adjuster named Parker who created it at a claim adjusters' convention, or (d) John Kenneth Galbraith.

Similarly, I have tried whenever possible to credit other collections from which laws have been collected. To save space, these have been abbreviated, and a key to these abbreviations appears at the end of the book following the entries for Z. However, six collections have been especially important to this effort, and they deserve mention here. These are the collections belonging to writer Fred Dyer (*FD* in the text), who was instrumental in getting the Center started; *Wall Street Journal* columnist Alan Otten (*A O*), who has done so much to popularize the idiom through his excellent articles on the subject; Jack Womeldorf of the Library of Congress (*JW*); Robert Specht (*RS*) of the RAND Corp.; and two computerized files: the John Erhman file at Stanford University (*J. E*), and the seminally important University of Arizona Computing Center collection, which was begun in January, 1974, by Conrad Schneiker and maintained by Gregg Townsend, Ed Logg, and others (*S. T. L.*).

Finally, one must thank all the people—dozens of them—who have helped with this effort. For their contributions, they have been made Fellows of the Murphy Center, a more than honorary title that might come in handy in a number of situations. For instance, should any of them ever need not to have to explain a nonproductive period in their life, they can simply say they are on a research fellowship from the Murphy Center. A list of Fellows appears on the very last pages of the book.

● **Abbott's Admonitions.** (1) If you have to ask, you're not entitled to know. (2) If you don't like the answer, you shouldn't have asked the question.

> (Charles C. Abbott, former dean of the Graduate School of Business Administration, University of Virginia. *AO.*)

● **Abrams's Advice.** When eating an elephant take one bite at a time.

> (General Creighton W. Abrams. *HE.*)

● **Accuracy, Rule of.** When working toward the solution of a problem, it always helps if you know the answer. *Advanced's Corollary:* Provided, of course, you know there is a problem.

> (Also known by other titles, such as the *Ultimate Law of Accuracy. AIC.*)

● **Acheson's Rule of the Bureaucracy.** A memorandum is written not to inform the reader but to protect the writer.

> (Dean Acheson, recalled by Harold P. Smith for *AO.*)

● **Acton's Law.** Power tends to corrupt, absolute power corrupts absolutely.

> (Lord Acton. *Co.*)

● **Ade's Law.** Anybody can win—unless there happens to be a second entry.

> (American humorist George Ade. *PQ.*)

● **Advertising Agency Song, The.**

> When your client's hopping mad,
> Put his picture in the ad.
> If he still should prove refractory
> Add a picture of his factory.

(Anonymous, from *Pith and Vinegar*, edited by William Cole, Simon & Schuster, 1969.)

● **Agnes Allen's Law.** Almost anything is easier to get into than out of.

(Agnes Allen was the wife of the famous historian Frederick Lewis Allen. When her husband was teaching at Yale, he encountered an ambitious student named Louis Zahner, who wanted to create and be remembered for a law of his own. Zahner worked on it and finally hit upon one that states: "If you play with anything long enough it will break." Inspired by his student, Allen then went to work on his own and came up with *Allen's Law*: "Everything is more complicated than it looks to most people." Agnes Allen then got into the act and proceeded to outdistance Zahner and her husband by creating the law that to this day carries her full name. Frederick Allen later wrote of his wife's law: ". . . at one stroke human wisdom had been advanced to an unprecedented degree." All of this was revealed in a column by Jack Smith in the *Los Angeles Times* after he had researched the question of who Murphy and Agnes Allen were. Needless to say, he proved Ms. Allen's law in the process.)

● **Airplane Law.** When the plane you are on is late, the plane you want to transfer to is on time.

A
3

● **Algren's Precepts.** Never eat at a place called Mom's. Never play cards with a man named Doc. And never lie down with a woman who's got more troubles than you.
(Nelson Algren, on "What Every Young Man Should Know.")

● **Allen's Axiom.** When all else fails, read the instructions. (*U/Scientific Collections.* Sometimes called *Cahn's Axiom.*)

● **Allen's Distinction.** The lion and the calf shall lie down together, but the calf won't get much sleep.

    (Woody Allen, from *Without Feathers*, Random House, 1977.)

● **Allen's Law of Civilization.** It is better for civilization to be going down the drain than to be coming up it.

    (Henry Allen, *The Washington Post.*)

● **Alley's Axiom.** Justice always prevails . . . three times out of seven!

    (*U.* The law itself comes from Michael J. Wagner of Miami.)

● **Allison's Precept.** The best simpleminded test of expertise in a particular area is an ability to win money in a series of bets on future occurrences in that area.

    (Graham Allison, the John F. Kennedy School of Government, to *AO.*)

● **Anderson's Law.** I have yet to see any problem, however complicated, which, when you looked at it in the right way, did not become still more complicated.

    (Writer Poul Anderson. *JW.*)

● **Andrews's Canoeing Postulate.** No matter which direction you start, it's always against the wind coming back.

    (Alfred Andrews. *JE.*)

● **Anthony's Law of Force.** Don't force it, get a larger hammer.

● **Anthony's Law of the Workshop.** Any tool, when dropped, will roll into the least accessible corner of the work-

shop. *Corollary:* On the way to the corner, any dropped tool will first always strike your toes.
> (*U/S.T.L.*)

● **Approval Seeker's Law.** Those whose approval you seek the most give you the least.
> (This is one of a number of laws created by Washington writer Rozanne Weissman. She is a natural-law writer whose style is characterized by restraint. Note that all of her laws bear situational titles.)

● **Army Axiom.** An order that can be misunderstood will be misunderstood.

● **Army Law.** If it moves, salute it; if it doesn't move, pick it up; and if you can't pick it up, paint it.
> (Both of these authentic Army items have been around at least since World War II, if not longer.)

● **Artz's Observation.** You can lead a whore to Vassar, but you can't make her think.
> (Frederick B. Artz, noted medieval historian. His observation was recorded in 1955. *JE.* This law is an obvious parody of Dorothy Parker's "You can lead a horticulture but you can't make her think.")

● **Ashley-Perry Statistical Axioms.** (1) Numbers are tools, not rules. (2) Numbers are symbols for things; the number and the thing are not the same. (3) Skill in manipulating numbers is a talent, not evidence of divine guidance. (4) Like other occult techniques of divination, the statistical method has a private jargon deliberately contrived to obscure its methods from nonpractitioners. (5) The product of an arithmetical computation is the answer to an equation; it is not the solution to a problem. (6)

Arithmetical proofs of theorems that do not have arithmetical bases prove nothing.

> (Drawn from Colonel G. O. Ashley's "A Declaration of Independence from the Statistical Method," *Air University Review*, March/April, 1964, and interpreted by R. L. Perry of the RAND Corp. *RS.*)

● **Asimov's Corollary** (to *Clarke's First Law*). When the lay public rallies round an idea that is denounced by distinguished but elderly scientists, and supports that idea with great fervor and emotion—the distinguished but elderly scientists are then, after all, right.

> (Isaac Asimov in his article "Asimov's Law" in the February, 1977, *Fantasy and Science Fiction Magazine.* One should also see *Clarke's Laws* and *Bartz's Law of Hokey Horsepuckery* for comparison. More laws by Asimov appear under *Robotics, The Three Laws of.*)

● **Astrology Law.** It's always the wrong time of the month. (Rozanne Weissman.)

● **Atwood's Fourteenth Corollary.** No books are lost by lending except those you particularly wanted to keep.

> (Alan Atwood, a programmer at the University Computing Center, University of Arizona. *S.T.L.*)

● **Avery, Sayings of.** (1) No ball game is ever much good unless the people involved hate each other. (2) On Monday mornings I am dedicated to the proposition that all men are created jerks. (3) Some performers on television appear to be horrible people, but when you finally get to know them in person, they turn out to be even worse. (4) There's such a thing as too much point on a pencil. (5) When there are two conflicting versions of a story, the wise course is to believe the one in which people appear at their worst.

(These are from the late H. Allen Smith's *Let the Crab-grass Grow,* Bernard Geis Associates, 1960. Avery is Smith's [presumably] fictional neighbor who is also responsible for the next two items. The second Avery item has shown up on various lists and may or may not have come from Smith's Avery.)

● **Avery's Law of Lubrication.** Everything needs a little oil now and then. (This as Smith finds Avery, a destructive do-it-yourselfer, pouring oil into the tiny hinges by which the bows of his glasses are attached to their frames.)

● **Avery's Observation.** It does not matter if you fall down as long as you pick up something from the floor while you get up.

● **Avery's Rule of Three.** Trouble strikes in series of threes, but when working around the house the next job after a series of three is not the fourth job—it's the start of a brand new series of three.

B

● **Baer's Quartet.** What's good politics is bad economics; what's bad politics is good economics; what's good economics is bad politics; what's bad economics is good politics.

(Eugene W. Baer of Middletown, R.I., to *AO*. Baer also allows that it can all be stated somewhat more compactly as "What's good politics is bad economics and vice versa, vice versa.")

● **Bagdikian's Law of Editor's Speeches.** The splendor of an editor's speech and the splendor of his newspaper are inversely related to the distance between the city in which he makes his speech and the city in which he publishes his paper.

(Ben Bagdikian, writer and press critic, Berkeley, Cal.)

● **Baker's Law.** Misery no longer loves company. Nowadays it insists on it.

(Columnist Russell Baker.)

● **Baldy's Law.** Some of it plus the rest of it is all of it.

(*U*. From the collection of laws assembled by Charles Wolf, Jr., of the RAND Corp.)

● **Barber's Laws of Backpacking.** (1) The integral of the gravitational potential taken around any loop trail you choose to hike always comes out positive. (2) Any stone in your boot always migrates against the pressure gradient to exactly the point of most pressure. (3) The weight of your pack increases in direct proportion to the amount of food you consume from it. If you run out of food, the pack weight goes on increasing anyway. (4) The

number of stones in your boot is directly proportional to the number of hours you have been on the trail. (5) The difficulty of finding any given trail marker is directly proportional to the importance of the consequences of failing to find it. (6) The size of each of the stones in your boot is directly proportional to the number of hours you have been on the trail. (7) The remaining distance to your chosen campsite remains constant as twilight approaches. (8) The net weight of your boots is proportional to the cube of the number of hours you have been on the trail. (9)

When you arrive at your campsite, it is full. (10) If you take your boots off, you'll never get them back on again. (11) The local density of mosquitos is inversely proportional to your remaining repellant.

> (Milt Barber, formerly a consultant at the Control Data Corp. *S.T.L.*)

● **Barrett's Laws of Driving.** (1) You can get *anywhere* in ten minutes if you go fast enough. (2) Speed bumps are of negligible effect when the vehicle exceeds triple the desired restraining speed. (3) The vehicle in front of you is traveling slower than you are. (4) This lane ends in 500 feet.

> (*U.* From John L. Shelton, President, Sigma Beta Communications, Inc., Dallas, Texas.)

● **Barr's Comment on Domestic Tranquility.** On a beautiful day like this it's hard to believe anyone can be unhappy—but we'll work on it.

> (Donald Barr, Highland Park, Ill., to *AO.*)

● **Barth's Distinction.** See *Benchley's Distinction.*

● **Bartz's Law of Hokey Horsepuckery.** The more ridiculous a belief system, the higher the probability of its success.

> (Wayne R. Bartz in his article "Keys to Success," *Human Behavior,* May, 1975.)

● **Baruch's Rule for Determining Old Age.** Old age is always fifteen years older than I am.

> (Bernard M. Baruch.)

● **Barzun's Laws of Learning.** (1) The simple but difficult arts of paying attention, copying accurately, following an argument, detecting an ambiguity or a false inference, testing guesses by summoning up contrary instances, organizing one's time and one's thought for study—all these arts . . . cannot be taught in the air but only through the difficulties of a defined subject; they cannot be taught in one course or one year, but must be acquired gradually in dozens of connections. (2) The analogy to athletics must be pressed until all recognize that in the exercise of Intellect those who lack the muscles, coordination, and will power can claim no place at the training table, let alone on the playing field.

(Jacques Barzun, from *The House of Intellect*, Harper & Row, 1959. Appeared in Martin's *MB* and a number of subsequent lists, including *S.T.L.,* where it appears in conjunction with *Forthoffer's Cynical Summary of Barzun's Laws*. [1] That which has not yet been taught directly can never be taught directly. [2] If at first you don't succeed, you will never succeed.)

● **Beardsley's Warning to Lawyers.** Beware of and eschew pompous prolixity.

(Charles A. Beardsley, the late president of the American Bar Association.)

● **Beauregard's Law.** When you're up to your nose, keep your mouth shut.

(Uttered by Henry Fonda in the role of Jack Beauregard in the film, *My Name Is Nobody. MLS.*)

● **Becker's Law.** It is much harder to find a job than to keep one.

(Jules Becker of Becker and Co., San Francisco, to *AO.* Becker, who claims that his law permeates industry as well as government, goes on to explain, ". . . once a person has been hired, inertia sets in, and the employer would rather settle for the current employee's incompetence and idiosyncrasies than look for a new employee.")

● **Beifeld's Principle.** The probability of a young man meeting a desirable and receptive young female increases by pyramidical progression when he is already in the company of (1) a date, (2) his wife, (3) a better looking and richer male friend.

(Ronald H. Beifeld, Philadelphia attorney, submitted to *AO* with alternative title, *The Law of Inverse Proportion of Social Intercourse.*)

● **Belle's Constant.** The ratio of time involved in work to time available for work is usually about 0.6.

(From a 1977 *JIR* article of the same title by Daniel McIvor and Oslen Belle, in which it is observed that knowledge of this constant is most useful in planning long-range projects. It is based on such things as an analysis of an eight-hour workday in which only 4.8 hours are actually spent working (or 0.6 of the time available), with the rest being spent on coffee breaks, bathroom visits, resting, walking, fiddling around, and trying to determine what to do next.)

● **Benchley's Distinction.** There may be said to be two classes of people in the world; those who constantly divide the people of the world into two classes and those who do not.

(Robert Benchley. This is often listed as *Barth's Distinction* [*S.T.L., JE,* etc.], but the Benchley quote is clearly much older.)

● **Bennett's Beatitudes.** (1) Blessed is he who has reached the point of no return and knows it, for he shall enjoy living. (2) Blessed is he who expects no gratitude, for he shall not be disappointed.

(W. C. Bennett, Trinity Avenue Presbyterian Church, Durham, N.C.)

● **Berkeley's Laws.** (1) The world is more complicated than most of our theories make it out to be. (2) Ignorance is no excuse. (3) Never decide to buy something while listening to the salesman. (4) Most problems have either many answers or no answer. Only a few problems have a single answer. (5) Most general statements are false, including this one. (6) An exception TESTS a rule; it NEVER PROVES it. (7) The moment you have worked out an answer, start checking it—it probably isn't right. (8) If there is an opportunity to make a mistake, sooner or later the mistake will be made. (9) Check the answer you have worked out once more—before you tell it to anybody.

> (Edmund C. Berkeley, "common sense" researcher and former editor of *Computers and Automation.* This is a mere sampling of Berkeley's to-the-point statements. They come from his article "Right Answers—A Short Guide for Obtaining Them," which appeared in the September, 1969, issue of *Computers and Automation.*)

● **Bernstein's Law.** A falling body always rolls to the most inaccessible spot.

> (Theodore M. Bernstein, from *The Careful Writer,* Atheneum, 1965. See also *Anthony's Law of the Workshop.*)

● **Berra's Law.** You can observe a lot just by watching.
(Yogi Berra. *RS.*)

● **Berson's Corollary of Inverse Distances.** The farther away from the entrance of the market (theater, or any other given location) that you have to park, the closer the space vacated by the car that pulls away as you walk up to the door.

> (Judith deMille Berson, Silver Spring, Md.)

● **Bicycle Law.** All bicycles weigh 50 pounds:
A 30-pound bicycle needs a 20-pound lock and chain.
A 40-pound bicycle needs a 10-pound lock and chain.
A 50-pound bicycle needs no lock and chain.
(*S.T.L.*)

● **Bicycling, First Law of.** No matter which way you ride, it's uphill and against the wind.

(*S.T.L.*)

● **Bill Babcock's Law.** If it can be borrowed and it can be broken, you will borrow it and you will break it.

(W. W. Chandler, Lyons, Kans., to *AO.*)

● **Billings Phenomenon.** The conclusions of most good operations research studies are obvious.

(Robert E. Machol, from "Principles of Operations Research" [*POR*]. The name refers to a well-known Billings story in which a farmer becomes concerned that his black horses are eating a lot more than his white horses. He does a detailed study of the situation and finds that he has more black horses than white horses. Machol points out that the obvious conclusions are not likely to be obvious a priori but obvious after the results are in. In other words, good research does not have to yield dramatic findings.)

● **Billings's Law.** Live within your income, even if you have to borrow to do so.

(19th Century American humorist Josh Billings. *PQ.*)

● **Blaauw's Law.** Established technology tends to persist in the face of new technology.

(Gerritt A. Blaauw, one of the designers of IBM's System/360. *JE.*)

● **Blanchard's Newspaper Obituary Law.** If you want your name spelled wrong, die.

(Al Blanchard, Washington bureau chief for *The Detroit News. AO.*)

● **Bloom's Law of the Profitable Inertia of Gold.** Certain things shouldn't be moved.

(Writer Murray Teigh Bloom, who first reported his discovery in his first book, *Money of Their Own,* Scribners, 1957. As he explained in a recent letter, "Once the Philadelphia Mint experimented and found $5.00 was lost by abrasion every time a million dollars worth of gold coin was handled. Just lifting the bags—each filled with $5,-000 worth of gold coin—to the truck resulted in a $5.00 loss; transferring them back to the mint caused another $5.00 loss. Letting the stuff rest quietly at Fort Knox instead of moving it around nervously to Sub-Treasuries makes us richer.")

● **Bok's Law.** If you think education is expensive—try ignorance.

(Derek Bok, president, Harvard University, quoted by Ann Landers in her column for March 26, 1978.)

● **Bolton's Law of Ascending Budgets.** Under current practices, both expenditures and revenues rise to meet each other, no matter which one may be in excess.

(Joe Bolton, Fellow of the RAND Graduate Institute. *RS.*)

● **Bombeck's Principles.** ■Any college that would take your son he should be too proud to go to. ■Know that a happy dieter has other problems. ■A man who checks out of the express lane with seven items is the same man who will wear Supp-Hose and park in the Reserved for Handicapped spaces. ■An old car that has served you so well will continue to serve you until you have just put four new tires under it and then will fall apart. ■A pregnancy will never occur when you have a low-paying job which you hate. ■An ugly carpet will last forever.

(Erma Bombeck, from her column of January 10, 1978.)

● **Bombeck's Rule of Medicine.** Never go to a doctor whose office plants have died.

(Erma Bombeck.)

● **Bonafede's Revelation.** The conventional wisdom is that power is an aphrodisiac. In truth, it's exhausting.

(Dom Bonafede in a February, 1977, article in the *Washingtonian* entitled "Surviving in Washington.")

● **Boob's Law.** You always find something the last place you look.

(Arthur Bloch's *Murphy's Law,* Price/Stern/Sloan Publishers Inc.)

● **Booker's Law.** An ounce of application is worth a ton of abstraction.

(*U/S.T.L.*)

● **Boozer's Revision.** A bird in the hand is dead.

(Rhonda Boozer, an elementary school pupil from Baltimore. This was produced when a teacher gave fourth and fifth graders the first half of an old adage and asked them to supply the second half. Other results of the adage improvement project according to an Associated Press report:

—"Don't put all your eggs in your pocket."
[Celestine Clark.]

—"Don't bite the hand that has your allowance in it."
[Lisa Tidler.]

—"If at first you don't succeed, blame it on the teacher."
[Stacey Bass.]

● **Boquist's Exception.** If for every rule there is an exception, then we have established that there is an exception to every rule. If we accept "For every rule there is an exception" as a rule, then we must concede that there may not be an exception after all, since the rule states that there is always the possibility of exception, and if we follow it to its logical end we must agree that there can be an exception to the rule that for every rule there is an exception.

    (Bill Boquist, San Francisco. *HW.*)

● **Boren's Laws of the Bureaucracy.** (1) When in doubt, mumble. (2) When in trouble, delegate. (3) When in charge, ponder.

    (James H. Boren, founder, president, and chairperson of the board of the International Association of Professional Bureaucrats [INATAPROBU].)

● **Borkowski's Law.** You can't guard against the arbitrary. (*U//C.*)

● **Boston's Irreversible Law of Clutter.** In any household, junk accumulates to fill the space available for its storage.

    (Bruce O. Boston, Fairfax, Va.)

● **Boultbee's Criterion.** If the converse of a statement is absurd, the original statement is an insult to the intelligence and should never have been said.

    (Arthur H. Boultbee, Greenwich, Conn., to *AO.* The author adds, "It is best applied to statements of politicians and TV pundits.")

● **Bowie's Theorem.** If an experiment works, you must be using the wrong equipment.

    (*U/RS.*)

● **Boyle's Laws.** (1) The success of any venture will be helped by prayer, even in the wrong denomination. (2) When things are going well, someone will inevitably experiment detrimentally. (3) The deficiency will never show itself during the dry runs. (4) Information travels more surely to those with a lesser need to know. (5) An original idea can never emerge from committee in the original. (6) When the product is destined to fail, the delivery system will perform perfectly. (7) The crucial memorandum will be snared in the out-basket by the paper clip of the overlying correspondence and go to file. (8) Success can be insured only by devising a defense against failure of the contingency plan. (9) Performance is directly affected by the perversity of inanimate objects. (10) If not controlled, work will flow to the competent man until he submerges. (11) The lagging activity in a project will invariably be found in the area where the highest overtime rates lie waiting. (12) Talent in staff work or sales will recurringly be interpreted as managerial ability. (13) The "think positive" leader tends to listen to his subordinates' premonitions only during the postmortems. (14) Clearly stated instructions will consistently produce multiple interpretations. (15) On successive charts of the same organization the number of boxes will never decrease.

> (Charles P. Boyle, Goddard Space Flight Center, NASA.)

● **Branch's First Law of Crisis.** The spirit of public service will rise, and the bureaucracy will multiply itself much faster, in time of grave national concern.

> (Taylor Branch, from his March, 1974, article in *Harper's* entitled "The Sunny Side of the Energy Crisis.")

● **Bribery, Mathematical Formula for.** $OG = PLR \times AEB$: The opportunity for graft equals the plethora of legal requirements multiplied by the number of architects, engineers, and builders.

> (Harold Birns, New York buildings commissioner, on the confusion of housing and building laws. *The New York Times,* October 2, 1963.)

● **Bridge, First Law of.** It's always the partner's fault.
(Sig Malek/*S.T.L.*)

● **Brien's First Law.** At some time in the life cycle of virtually every organization, its ability to succeed in spite of itself runs out.

> (Richard H. Brien, "The Managerialization of Higher Education," from *Educational Record,* Summer, 1970. Appears in *MB, S.T.L.,* etc.)

● **Broder's Law.** Anybody that wants the presidency so much that he'll spend two years organizing and campaigning for it is not to be trusted with the office.

> (David Broder in *The Washington Post,* July 19, 1973. *JW.*)

● **Broken Mirror Law.** Everyone breaks more than the seven-year-bad-luck allotment to cover rotten luck throughout an entire lifetime.

> (Rozanne Weissman.)

● **Brontosaurus Principle.** Organizations can grow faster than their brains can manage them in relation to their environment and to their own physiology: when this occurs, they are an endangered species.

> (Thomas K. Connellan, president of The Management Group, Inc. of Ann Arbor, Mich., from his 1976 book *The Brontosaurus Principle: A Manual for Corporate Survival,* Prentice-Hall.)

● **Brooks's Law.** Adding manpower to a late software project makes it later.

> (Frederick P. Brooks, Jr., from *The Mythical Man-Month: Essays on Software Engineering,* Addison-Wesley, 1974. *S.T.L.*)

● **Brown's Law. [J.]** Too often I find that the volume of paper expands to fill the available briefcases.

(Governor Jerry Brown, quoted in *State Government News,* March, 1973. *AO.*)

● **Brown's Law. [S.]** Never offend people with style when you can offend them with substance.
(Sam Brown, from *The Washington Post,* January 26, 1977. *JW.*)

● **Brown's Law of Business Success.** Our customer's paperwork is profit. Our own paperwork is loss.
(Tony Brown, programmer at the Control Data Corp. *S.T.L.*)

● **Bruce-Briggs's Law of Traffic.** At any level of traffic, any delay is intolerable.
(Barry Bruce-Briggs of the Hudson Institute, from his article "Mass Transportation and Minority Transportation" in *The Public Interest.* In explaining his law he adds, "It is amusing for someone accustomed to the traffic in New York to hear residents of places like Houston and Atlanta complain about congestion on the highways. Imagine, in rush hour they have to slow down to 35 miles an hour!")

● **Brumfit's Law.** The critical mass of any do-it-yourself explosive is never less than half a bucketful.
(*ASF* letter from Eric Frank Russell, who explained that the law was first demonstrated by Emmanuel Brumfit. Beginning with a half ounce of homemade gunpowder, Brumfit attempted to see what would happen if he lit it. When nothing happened he went on mixing and adding until, on his fifty-fourth match, he reached exactly a half a bucketful and "went out the window without bothering to open it.")

● **Buchwald's Law.** As the economy gets better, everything else gets worse.

(Art Buchwald, *Time,* January, 1972. *JW.*)

● **Bucy's Law.** Nothing is ever accomplished by a reasonable man.

(Fred Bucy, Texas Instruments Inc.)

● **Bugger Factor (sometimes Bouguerre).** See *Finagle.*

● **Bureaucracy, The Second Order Rule of.** The more directives you issue to solve a problem, the worse it gets.

(Jack Robertson, *Electronic News,* quoted in *New Engineer,* November, 1976.)

● **Bureaucratic Cop-Out #1.** You should have seen it when *I* got it.

(Marshall L. Smith, WMAL, Washington, D.C.)

Bureaucratic Laws, Creeds, and Mottoes. Here is a select collection of items that have been collected in recent years from the halls of the federal government. None is attributed to anyone in particular and all were found hanging from office walls or partitions, where they were presumably placed for their inspirational value:

When you're up to your ass in alligators, it is difficult to keep your mind on the fact that your primary objective is to drain the swamp.

* * *

A. Running a project in this office is like mating elephants—it takes a great deal of time and effort to get on top of things; B. The whole affair is always accompanied by a great deal of noise and confusion, the culmination of which is heralded by loud trumpeting; C. After which, nothing comes of the effort for two years.

* * *

The road to hell is paved with good intentions. And littered with sloppy analysis!

* * *

B

If you want something done, ask a busy person.

● **Burns's Balance.** If the assumptions are wrong, the conclusions aren't likely to be very good.
(Robert E. Machol, from "Principles of Operations Research." The principle refers to the late radio comedian Robert Burns and his method for weighing hogs. Burns got a perfectly symmetrical plank and balanced it across a sawhorse. He would then put the hog on one end of the plank and began piling rocks on the other end until the plank was again perfectly balanced across the sawhorse. At this point he would carefully guess the weight of the rocks.)

● **Bustlin' Billy's Bogus Beliefs.** (1) The organization of any program reflects the organization of the people who develop it. (2) There is no such thing as a "dirty capitalist," only a capitalist. (3) Anything is possible, but nothing is easy. (4) Capitalism can exist in one of only two states—welfare or warfare. (5) I'd rather go whoring than warring. (6) History proves nothing. (7) There is nothing so unbecoming on the beach as a wet kilt. (8) A little humility is arrogance. (9) A lot of what appears to be progress is just so much technological rococo.

> (Bill Gray, formerly of the Control Data Corp., friend of compilers of *S.T.L.*)

● **Butler's Law of Progress.** All progress is based on a universal innate desire on the part of every organism to live beyond its income.

> (Samuel Butler, *Note-Books.*)

● **Bye's First Law of Model Railroading.** Any time you wish to demonstrate something, the number of faults is proportional to the number of viewers.

● **Bye's Second Law of Model Railroading.** The desire for modeling a prototype is inversely proportional to the decline of the prototype.

> (*U/S.T.L.*)

C

- **Caen's Law.** All American cars are basically Chevrolets. (Herb Caen of the *San Francisco Chronicle*. RS.)

- **Calkins's Law of Menu Language.** The number of adjectives and verbs that are added to the description of a menu item is in inverse proportion to the quality of the resulting dish.
(John Calkins of Washington, D.C., in a letter to *The Washington Post,* May, 1977. *JW.*)

- **Camp's Law.** A coup that is known in advance is a coup that does not take place.
(The law that was reported by *AO* was alluded to by former CIA Director William Colby in a briefing for reporters. It is apparently known throughout the intelligence community and, Otten presumes, was named after a secret operation [operator?] named Camp.)

- **Canada Bill Jones's Motto.** It is morally wrong to allow suckers to keep their money.

- **Canada Bill Jones's Supplement.** A Smith and Wesson beats four aces.
(*U/S.T.L.*)

- **Carson's Consolation.** No experiment is ever a complete failure. It can always be used as a bad example.
(*U.* From a list entitled "Wisdom from the Giants of Science," found on a wall at National Institutes of Health, *MLS.* This has also been reported as *Carlson'sConsolation.*)

● **Chamberlain's Laws.** (1) The big guys always win. (2) Everything tastes more or less like chicken.

> (Jeffery F. Chamberlain, Rochester, N.Y., in a letter to *Verbatim.*)

● **Character and Appearance, Law of.** People don't change; they only become more so.

> (John Bright-Holmes, editor, George Allen & Unwin [Publishers] Ltd., London.)

● **Chatauqua Boulevard Law.** Just when I finally figure out where it's at . . . somebody moves it.

> (Sign in window, Chautauqua Boulevard and Coast Highway, Pacific Palisades, Cal. Collected by *RS.*)

● **Checkbook Balancer's Law.** In matters of dispute, the bank's balance is always smaller than yours.

> (Rozanne Weissman.)

● **Cheops's Law.** Nothing ever gets built on schedule or within budget.

> (*S.T.L.*)

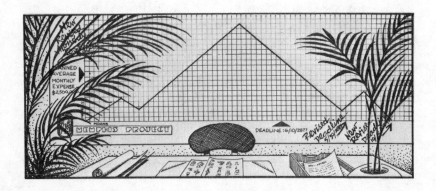

● **Chili Cook's Secret.** If your next pot of chili tastes better, it probably is because of something left out, rather than added.
(Hal John Wimberley, editor and publisher, *The Goat Gap Gazette,* Houston, Texas.)

● **Chinese Fortune Cookie Law.** Inappropriate fortunes always find the right person; and you always want more three hours later.
(Rozanne Weissman.)

● **Chisholm Effect—Basic Laws of Frustration, Mishap, and Delay.** *1st Law of Human Interaction.* If anything can go wrong, it will. *Corollary:* If anything just can't go wrong, it will anyway. *2d Law of Human Interaction.* When things are going well, something will go wrong. *Corollary:* When things just can't get any worse, they will. *Corollary 2:* Anytime things appear to be going better, you have overlooked something. *3rd Law of Human Interaction.* Purposes, as understood by the purposer, will be judged otherwise by others. *Corollary:* If you explain so clearly that nobody can misunderstand, somebody will. *Corollary 2:* If you do something which you are sure will meet with everybody's approval, somebody won't like it. *Corollary 3:* Procedures devised to implement the purpose won't quite work.
(Francis P. Chisholm was professor of English and chairman of the department at Wisconsin State College in River Falls for many years. His original article, "The Chisholm Effect," was published a number of years ago in a magazine called *motive.* Because of their resemblance to *Murphy's* and *Finagle's Laws,* his *1st and 2d Laws* are not well remembered today, but his *3rd,* complete with *Corollaries,* is one of the most quoted of modern laws. Sometimes the *3rd* is quoted with a *Corollary 4:* "No matter how long or how many times you explain, no one is listening." This may have been written by someone other than Chisholm and added after the original article.)

● **Christmas Morning, The First Discovery of.** Batteries not included.

(From the side panel of a toy box. Small print.)

● **Ciardi's Poetry Law.** Whenever in time, and wherever in the universe, any man speaks or writes in any detail about the technical management of a poem, the resulting irascibility of the reader's response is a constant.

(John Ciardi, in his "Manner of Speaking" column in *Saturday Review,* February 13, 1965. He created it in response to the reader outcry over some columns in which he wrote about the technical side of poetry.)

● **Clarke's Laws.** (1) When a distinguished but elderly scientist states that something is possible, he is almost certainly right. When he states that something is impossible, he is very probably wrong. (2) The only way to discover the limits of the possible is to go beyond them to the impossible. (3) Any sufficiently advanced technology is indistinguishable from magic.

(Arthur C. Clarke, from his book *Profiles of the Future,* Harper & Row, 1962. In illustrating the first law he uses the example of Lord Rutherford, who ". . . more than any other man laid bare the internal structure of the atom" but who also made fun of those who predicted the harnessing of atomic power. Clarke also elaborates on the meaning of the word "elderly" in the first law. He says that in physics, astronautics, and mathematics it means over thirty, but that in some fields "senile decay" is postponed into the forties. He adds, "There are, of course, glorious exceptions; but as every good researcher just out of college knows, scientists of over fifty are good for nothing but board meetings, and should at all costs be kept out of the laboratory!")

● **Clark's First Law of Relativity.** No matter how often you trade dinner or other invitations with in-laws, you will lose a small fortune in the exchange. *Corollary 1 on Clark's First:* Don't try it: you cannot drink enough of your in-laws' booze to get even before the liver fails.

(Jackson Clark, Cuero, Texas, to *AO.*)

● **Clark's Law.** It's always darkest just before the lights go out.

(Alex Clark, Lyndon B. Johnson School, Texas, at a RAND Graduate Institute meeting. *RS.*)

● **Cleveland's Highway Law.** Highways in the worst need of repair naturally have low traffic counts, which results in low priority for repair work.

(Named for Representative Jim Cleveland of New Hampshire. Its truth was revealed some years ago during Public Works Appropriations hearings as highway aid to New Hampshire was being reduced. *JMcC.*)

● **Cliff-hanger Theorem.** Each problem solved introduces a new unsolved problem.

(Posted in U.S. Department of Labor. *TO'B.*)

● **Clopton's Law.** For every credibility gap there is a gullibility fill.

(Richard Clopton. *PQ.*)

● **Clyde's Law.** If you have something to do, and you put it off long enough, chances are someone else will do it for you.

(Clyde F. Adams, Auburn, Ala.)

● **Cohen's Choice.** Everybody's gotta be someplace.
(Comedian Myron Cohen. *MLS.*)

● **Cohen's Law. [J.]** What really matters is the name you succeed in imposing on the facts—not the facts themselves.

(Jerome Cohen, Harvard Law School professor, quoted in *Time,* June 7, 1971.)

● **Cohen's Laws of Politics. [M.]** *Cohen's Law of Alienation:* Nothing can so alienate a voter from the political system as backing a winning candidate. *Cohen's Law of Ambition:* At any one time, thousands of borough councilmen, school board members, attorneys, and businessmen—as well as congressmen, senators, and governors—are dreaming of the White House, but few, if any of them, will make it. *Cohen's Law of Attraction:* Power attracts people but it cannot hold them. *Cohen's Law of Competition:* The more qualified candidates who are available, the more likely the compromise will be on the candidate whose main qualification is a nonthreatening incompetence. *Cohen's Law of Inside Dope:* There are many inside dopes in politics and government. *Cohen's Law on Lawmaking:* Those who express random thoughts to legislative committees are often surprised and appalled to find themselves the instigators of law. *Cohen's Law of Permanence:* Political power is as permanent as today's newspaper. Ten years from now, few will know or care who the most powerful man in any state was today. *Cohen's Law of Practicality:* Courses of action which run only to be justified in terms of practicality ultimately prove destructive and impractical. *Cohen's Law of Secrecy:* The best way to publicize a governmental or political action is to attempt to hide it. *Cohen's Law of Wealth:* Victory goes to the candidate with the most accumulated or contributed wealth who has the financial sources to convince the middle class and poor that he will be on their side. *Cohen's Law of Wisdom:* Wisdom is considered a sign of weakness by the powerful because a wise man can lead without power but only a powerful man can lead without wisdom.

(Mark B. Cohen, member, House of Representatives,

Commonwealth of Pennsylvania. Cohen writes his own as well as collects other people's political laws.)

● **Cohn's Law.** The more time you spend in reporting on what you are doing, the less time you have to do anything. Stability is achieved when you spend all your time doing nothing but reporting on the nothing you are doing.
(*U/TO'B.*)

● **Cole's Law.** Thinly sliced cabbage.
(*S.T.L.*)

● **Colson's Law.** If you've got them by the balls, their hearts and minds will follow.
(From a poster *alleged* to have hung in the office of a key Nixon aide. *MLS.*)

● **Comins's Law.** People will accept your idea much more readily if you tell them Benjamin Franklin said it first.
(David H. Comins, Manchester, Conn. *HW.*)

● **Committee Rules.** (1) Never arrive on time, or you will be stamped a beginner. (2) Don't say anything until the meeting is half over; this stamps you as being wise. (3) Be as vague as possible; this prevents irritating the others. (4) When in doubt, suggest that a subcommittee be appointed. (5) Be the first to move for adjournment; this will make you popular—it's what everyone is waiting for.
(Harry Chapman, *Think. FD.*)

● **Commoner's Three Laws of Ecology.** (1) No action is without side effects. (2) Nothing ever goes away. (3) There is no free lunch.
(Barry Commoner. See also *Crane's Law.*)

● **Compensation Corollary.** An experiment may be considered successful if no more than half of the data must be discarded to obtain correspondence with your theory.

(From list, "Wisdom from the Giants of Science," *MLS* collection.)

● **Computability Applied to Social Sciences, Law of.** If at first you don't succeed, transform your data set.

(*U//E.*)

● **Computer Maxim.** To err is human but to really foul things up requires a computer.

(*The Farmers' Almanac,* 1978 edition.)

● **Computer Programming, Laws of.** (1) Any given program, when running, is obsolete. (2) Any given program costs more and takes longer. (3) If a program is useful, it will have to be changed. (4) If a program is useless, it will have to be documented. (5) Any given program will expand to fill all available memory. (6) The value of a program is proportional to the weight of its output. (7) Program complexity grows until it exceeds the capability of the programmer who must maintain it. (8) Make it possible for programmers to write programs in English, and you will find that programmers cannot write in English.

(*SIGPLAN Notices,* Vol. 2, No. 2. *JE.*)

● **Connally's Rule.** Wage and price controls cause inequities, ineffiencies, distortions, and venality, and therefore should be invoked only when necessary.

(John B. Connally. Culled from speech by *JMcC.*)

● **Connolly's Law of Cost Control.** The price of any product produced for a government agency will be not less than the square of the initial Firm Fixed-Price Contract.

(Ray Connolly, Washington bureau manager and columnist, *Electronics* magazine.)

● **Connolly's Rule for Political Incumbents.** Short-term success with voters on any side of a given issue can be guaranteed by creating a long-term special study commission made up of at least three divergent interest groups.
(Ray Connolly, *Electronics.*)

● **Considine's Law.** Whenever one word or letter can change the entire meaning of a sentence, the probability of an error being made will be in direct proportion to the embarrassment it will cause.
(Reporter and author Bob Considine. Recalled by Bill Gold in his *Washington Post* column the day after a reader had written in to report that the paper had stated that a woman was "sex weeks pregnant.")

● **Cooke's Law.** In any decision situation, the amount of relevant information available is inversely proportional to the importance of the decision.
(*U.* Michael T. Minerath, West Haven, Conn.)

● **Coolidge's Immutable Observation.** When more and more people are thrown out of work, unemployment results.
(Calvin Coolidge, from Leonard C. Lewin's *Treasury of American Political Humor,* Dial, 1964.)

● **Coomb's Law.** If you can't measure it, I'm not interested.
(*U* from an article in *Human Behavior* called "Peter's People" by Lawrence J. Peter, August, 1976.)

● **Corcoran's Law of Packrattery.** All files, papers, memos, etc., that you save will never be needed until such time as they are disposed of, when they will become essential and indispensible.

(John Corcoran, Washington writer and television personality. He also wrote the next item, which appeared in the *Washingtonian* magazine, March, 1974.)

● **Corcoroni's Laws of Bus Transportation.** (1) The bus that left the stop just before you got there is your bus. (2) The amount of time you have to wait for a bus is directly proportional to the inclemency of the weather. (3) All buses heading in the opposite direction drive off the face of the earth and never return. (4) If you anticipate bus delays by leaving your house thirty minutes early, your bus will arrive as soon as you reach the bus stop or when you light up a cigarette, whichever comes first. (5) The last rush-hour express bus to your neighborhood leaves five minutes before you get off work. (6) Bus schedules are arranged so your bus will arrive at the transfer point precisely one minute after the connecting bus has left. (7) Any bus that can be the wrong bus will be the wrong bus. All others are out of service or full.

(John Corcoran, aka Corcoroni, *The Washingtonian,* March, 1974.)

● **Cornuelle's Law.** Authority tends to assign jobs to those least able to do them.

(Richard C. Cornuelle/*S.T.L.*)

● **Crane's Law.** There ain't no such thing as a free lunch. (Burton Crane, in *The Sophisticated Investor,* Simon and Schuster, 1959. See also *Commoner's Laws, Solis's Amendment to Crane's Law.*)

● **Crane's Rule.** There are three ways to get something done: do it yourself, hire someone, or forbid your kids to do it. (Monta Crane, in *Sunshine Magazine* and requoted in *Reader's Digest,* June, 1977.)

● **Cripp's Law.** When traveling with children on one's holidays, at least one child of any number of children will request a rest room stop exactly half way between any two given rest areas.

> (Mervyn Cripps, St. Catherines, Ontario, in a letter to *Verbatim.*)

● **Culshaw's First Principle of Recorded Sound.** Anything, no matter how bad, will sound good if played back at a very high level for a short time.

> (John Culshaw, in his column for *High Fidelity Magazine,* November, 1977.)

● **Curley's Law.** As long as they spell the name right.
> (Named for the famous Boston mayor. From Vic Gold's *P.R. as in President,* Doubleday, 1977.)

● **Cushman's Law.** A fail-safe circuit will destroy others.
> (*U/S.T.L.*)

● **Cutler Webster's Law.** There are two sides to every argument, unless a person is personally involved, in which case there is only one.
> (*U/RS.*)

● **Czecinski's Conclusion.** There is only one thing worse than dreaming you are at a conference and waking up to find that you are at a conference: and that is the conference where you can't fall asleep.

> (Adapted from a translation of a letter from Tadeusz Czecinski to a Warsaw newspaper. *RS.*)

D

● **Darrow's Observation.** History repeats itself. That's one of the things wrong with history.
(Clarence Darrow.)

● **Darwin's Observation.** Nature will tell you a direct lie if she can.
(Charles Darwin.)

● **Dave's Law of Advice.** Those with the best advice offer no advice.

● **Davidson's Maxim.** Democracy is that form of government where everybody gets what the majority deserves.
(James Dale Davidson, executive director of the National Taxpayer's Union. *JMcC.*)

● **Dave's Rule of Street Survival.** Speak softly and own a big, mean Doberman.
(Dave Miliman, Baltimore.)

● **Davis's Basic Law of Medicine.** Pills to be taken in twos always come out of the bottle in threes.
(Robert Davis. *AO.*)

● **Davis's Laws.** (1) Writers desire to be paid, authors desire recognition. (2) The further an individual is from the poorhouse, the more expert one becomes on the ghetto. (3) In business, price increases as service declines. (4) On soap operas all whites are in personal touch with (a) a doctor and (b) a lawyer.
(James L. Davis, Washington, D.C.)

● **Dawes-Bell Law.** Whereas in many branches of economic activity employment depends on the number of job openings available, in the public service, as also in the advertising business, social science investigation, and university administration, the level of employment regularly depends on the number of men available and devoting their time to the creation of job opportunities.

> (First reported in *The McLandress Dimension* by Mark Epernay, Houghton Mifflin, 1962. See also *McLandress Dimension.*)

● **Dean's Law of the District of Columbia.** Washington is a much better place if you are asking questions rather than answering them.

> (John Dean, former counsel to President Nixon, on the occasion of beginning his syndicated radio interview show.)

● **DeCaprio's Rule.** Everything takes more time and money.

> (Annie DeCaprio, High Bridge, N.J. *HW*. Note similarity to *Cheops's Law.*)

● **Deitz's Law of Ego.** The fury engendered by the misspelling of a name in a column is in direct ratio to the obscurity of the mentionee.

> (Alan Deitz of the American Newspaper Publishers Association to *AO* on the misspelling of his name in *The Wall Street Journal.*)

● **Dennis's Principles of Management by Crisis.** (1) To get action out of management, it is necessary to create the illusion of a crisis in the hope it will be acted on. (2) Management will select actions or events and convert them to crises. It will then over-react. (3) Management is incapable of recognizing a true crisis. (4) The squeaky hinge gets the oil.

(Gene Franklin, from his article in *Computers and Automation. JE.*)

● **Dhawan's Laws for the Non-Smoker.** (1) The cigarette smoke always drifts in the direction of the non-smoker regardless of the direction of the breeze. (2) The amount of pleasure derived from a cigarette is directly proportional to the number of the non-smokers in the vicinity. (3) A smoker is always attracted to the non-smoking section. (4) The life of a cigarette is directly proportional to the intensity of the protests from the non-smokers.
(Raj K. Dhawan, West Covina, Cal.)

● **Dibble's First Law of Sociology.** Some do, some don't.
(Letter to *Verbatim* from Jeffery F. Chamberlain.)

● **Dieter's Law.** Food that tastes the best has the highest number of calories.
(Rozanne Weissman.)

● **Dijkstra's Prescription for Programming Inertia.** If you don't know what your program is supposed to do, you'd better not start writing it.
(*JE* carries this with the notation: "Stanford Computer Science Colloquium, April 18, 1975.")

● **Dilwether's Law of Delay.** When people have a job to do, particularly a vital but difficult one, they will invariably put it off until the last possible moment, and *most* of them will put it off even longer.
(Gordon L. Becker, counsel, Exxon Corp. *AO.*)

● **Diogenes's First Dictum.** The more heavily a man is supposed to be taxed, the more power he has to escape being taxed.

● **Diogenes's Second Dictum.** If a taxpayer thinks he can cheat safely, he probably will.
(*S.T.L.*)

● **Dirksen's Three Laws of Politics.** (1) Get elected. (2) Get reelected. (3) Don't get mad, get even.
(Senator Everett Dirksen. Recalled by Harry N. D. Fisher for *AO*. See also *Johnson's "Prior" Laws of Politics.*)

● **Dirksen's Version of an Old Saw.** The oil can is mightier than the sword.
(Senator Dirksen again. This was contained in Donald Rumsfeld's collection of laws.)

● **Displaced Hassle, Principle of.** To beat the bureaucracy, make your problem their problem.
(Marshall L. Smith, who is also law-collector *MLS.*)

● **Distance, Law of.** Happiness is in direct proportion to the distance from the home office. *Contradictory Corollary:* The diner who is furthest from the kitchen is a nervous eater.
(Stated by Al Blanchard, *The Detroit News,* in his column for September 16, 1977.)

● **Dobbins's Law.** When in doubt, use a bigger hammer.
(A variation of *Anthony's Law of Force,* probably earlier.)

● **Domino Theory II.** If you disregard the advice of Gen. Douglas MacArthur and go into the quicksand of an Asian country, like a domino you will fall into the quicksand of another Asian country next to it.
(Representative Andrew Jacobs, Jr., D-Ind., who created it about the time of the U.S. incursion into Cambodia.)

● **Donohue's Law.** What's worth doing is worth doing for money.

> (Joseph Donohue. *JW.*)

● **Donsen's Law.** The specialist learns more and more about less and less until, finally, he knows everything about nothing; whereas the generalist learns less and less about more and more until, finally, he knows nothing about everything.

> (*U/"LSP."*)

● **Dorm Room Living, Laws of.** (1) The amount of trash accumulated within the space occupied is exponentially proportional to the number of living bodies that enter and leave within any given amount of time. (2) Since no matter can be created or destroyed (excluding nuclear and cafeteria substances), as one attempts to remove unwanted material (i.e., trash) from one's living space, the remaining material mutates so as to occupy 30 to 50 percent more than its original volume. *Corollary:* Dust breeds. (3) The odds are 6:5 that if one has late classes, one's roommate will have the *earliest* possible classes. *Corollary 1*: One's roommate (who has early classes) has an alarm clock that is louder than God's own. *Corollary 2*: When one has an early class, one's roommate will invariably enter the space late at night and suddenly become hyperactive, ill, violent, or all three.

> (*U.* Part of a larger collection originating at East Russell Hall, University of Georgia, Athens.)

● **Douglas's Law of Practical Aeronautics.** When the weight of the paperwork equals the weight of the plane, the plane will fly.

> (Airplane-builder Donald Douglas, who articulated it for Jerome S. Katzin of La Jolla, Cal., who passed it along to *AO.*)

● **Dow's Law.** In a hierarchical organization, the higher the level, the greater the confusion.

(*U/S.T.L.*)

● **Dror Law, First.** While the difficulties and dangers of problems tend to increase at a geometric rate, the knowledge and manpower qualified to deal with these problems tend to increase at an arithmetic rate.

● **Dror Law, Second.** While human capacities to shape the environment, society, and human beings are rapidly increasing, policymaking capabilities to use those capacities remain the same.

(Yehezkel Dror, Israeli policy analyst at Hebrew University, from "Policy Sciences: Developments and Implications," RAND Corp. Paper P–4321, March, 1970.)

● **Drucker, The Sayings of Chairman Peter.** (1) If you have too many problems, maybe you should go out of business. There is no law that says a company must last forever. (2) As to the idea that advertising motivates people, remember the Edsel. (3) The only things that evolve by themselves in an organization are disorder, friction, and malperformance. (4) We know nothing about motivation. All we can do is write books about it. (5) Marketing is a fashionable term. The sales manager becomes a marketing vice-president. But a gravedigger is still a gravedigger even when he is called a mortician—only the price of burial goes up. (6) Fast personal decisions are likely to be wrong. (7) Strong people always have strong weaknesses. (8) Start with what is right rather than with what is acceptable. (9) We always remember best the irrelevant. (10) When a subject becomes totally obsolete we make it a required course. (11) Medicare and Medicaid are the greatest measures yet devised to make the world safe for clerks. (12) We may now be nearing the end of our hundred-year belief in Free Lunch. (See *Commoner's* and *Crane's Laws*.) (13)

Look at governmental programs for the past fifty years. Every single one—except for warfare—achieved the exact opposite of its announced goal. (14) The computer is a moron. (15) The main impact of the computer has been the provision of unlimited jobs for clerks.

> (Selected by the author from *Drucker: The Man Who Invented the Corporate Society* by John J. Tarrant, Cahners Books, Inc., 1976.)

● **Dude's Law of Duality.** Of two possible events, only the undesired one will occur.

> (This can be expressed mathematically as:
>
> $$A \cap B^u = B \ [1]$$
> $$A^u \cap B = A \ [2]$$
>
> where A and B are possible outcomes, where the superscript ^{u} denotes the undesired outcome, and where $\cap$ means either/or.
> ([From Walter Mulé's article, "Beyomd Murphy's Law," in *Northliner*. Mulé says the law was named for Sam Dude, whose genius was cut short by a skydiving accident that occurred just after he was forced to choose between two types of parachute.])

● **Duggan's Law.** To every Ph.D there is an equal and opposite Ph.D.

> (B. Duggan, quoted from one of Robert Specht's quote-laden calendars, *1970 Expectation of Days. RS.* This law helps explain why it is so easy to find expert witnesses to totally contradict each other.)

● **Dunne's Law.** The territory behind rhetoric is too often mined with equivocation.

> (John Gregory Dunne, "To Die Standing," *The Atlantic,* June, 1971.)

● **Dunn's Discovery.** The shortest measurable interval of time is the time between the moment I put a little extra aside for a sudden emergency and the arrival of that emergency.

(Marvin Dunn, quoted in the *Louisville Courier-Journal.*)

● **du Pont's Laws.** A COMPENDIUM OF HELPFUL RULES GOVERNING THE LEGISLATIVE PROCESS NOT TO BE FOUND IN JEFFERSON'S MANUAL OF RULES AND PRACTICES OF THE HOUSE OF REPRESENTATIVES. (1) Vote as an individual; lemmings end up falling off cliffs. Camaraderie is no substitute for common sense, and being your own man will make you sleep better. (2) The speed at which the legislative process seems to work is in inverse proportion to your enthusiasm for the bill. If you want a bill to move quickly, committee hearings, the rules committee, and legislative procedures appear to be roadblocks to democracy. If you do not want the bill to pass, such procedures are essential to furthering representative government, etc., etc. (3) The titles of bills—like those of Marx Brothers movies—often have little to do with the substance of the legislation. Particularly deceptive are bills containing title buzz words such as *emergency, reform, service, relief,* or *special.* Often the *emergency* is of the writer's imagination; the *reform,* a protection of vested interest; the *service,* self-serving; the *relief,* an additional burden on the taxpayer; and the *special,* something that otherwise shouldn't be passed. (4) Sometimes the best law of all is no law at all. Not all the world's ills are susceptible to legislative correction. (5) When voting on appropriations bills, more is not necessarily better. It is as wasteful to have a B–1 bomber in every garage as it is to have a welfare program for every conceivable form of deprivation. (6) The Crusades ended several centuries ago after killing thousands of people. The most important issues arouse intense passions. Earmuffs to block the shouting are inappropriate, but filter the feedback. Joining a cause and leading a constituency are not mutually exclusive, but neither are they necessarily synonymous. Neither welfare nor profits are "obscene." (7) "Beware the [lobbyist], my son, the jaws that bite, the claws that snatch" (with thanks to Lewis Carroll). No matter how noble the cause or well meaning its professional advocates, lobbyists are still paid to get results. They're subject to errors in judgment, shortcomings in motives, and most of them don't even vote in your district. (8) Mirror, mirror on the wall, who's the fairest one of all? The press is hopelessly biased or genuinely fair, depending upon whose views are being misquoted, misrepresented, or misunderstood. (9) If you are concerned about being criticized—you're in the wrong job. However you vote, and whatever you do, somebody will be out there telling you that you are: (a) wrong, (b) insensitive, (c) a bleeding heart, (d) a pawn of somebody else, (e) too wishy-washy, (f) too unwilling to compromise, (g) all of the above—consistency is not required of critics.

(Governor Pierre S. du Pont of Delaware, who wrote them when he was a congressman. The laws were written for incoming members, about whom he said in his introduction to the laws: "A freshman Congressman trying to do his job properly is similar to a quarterback trying to throw a 60-yard pass with a deflated football. The only difference is the quarterback knows there is no air in the ball—the freshman Congressman doesn't even know what game he is playing." See also *Fifth Rule.*)

● **Durant's Discovery.** One of the lessons of history is that nothing is often a good thing to do and always a clever thing to say.

(Will Durant, from an item in the November, 1972, *Reader's Digest* quoting Derek Gill's article on Durant in *Modern Maturity.*)

● **Durrell's Parameter.** The faster the plane, the narrower the seats.

(John H. Durrell of Mason, Ohio, in a letter to the editor, *The Wall Street Journal,* March 15, 1976.)

● **Dyer's Law.** A continuing flow of paper is sufficient to continue the flow of paper.

      (Professor John M. Dyer, director, International Finance and Marketing Program, University of Miami, Coral Gables, Fla. *FD.*)

● **Ear's Law.** Before a party or a trip, if it can, it will let rip. (From the "Ear" column in the *Washington Star*. It was recalled in print when the Carters' hot-water heater burst on their last day in Plains before leaving for the Inauguration.)

● **Economists' Laws.** (1) What men learn from history is that men do not learn from history. (2) If on an actuarial basis there is a 50/50 chance that something will go wrong, it will actually go wrong nine times in ten.
(*2p.?*)

● **Edington's Theory.** Hypotheses multiply so as to fill the gaps in factual knowledge concerning biological phenomena.
(Named for C. W. Edington, but first explained by James D. Regan in the April, 1963, issue of the *Journal of Irreproducible Results*. Although created for biological phenomena, it was noted in the original article that it applied in other scientific areas as well.)

● **Editorial Correction, Law of.** Anyone nit-picking enough to write a letter of correction to an editor doubtless deserves the error that provoked it.
(This law was created by Alvin Toffler and published in the *New York Times Magazine* on April 7, 1968. It was written in response to an article by Harold Faber on laws, i.e., "Faber's Law—If There Isn't a Law, There Will Be." Toffler said, in part, that a law credited to Anthony Toffler called the *Law of Raspberry Jam* was originated by Stan-

ley Edgar Hyman. He added, "Not only is my name not Anthony—which I regret—but I heartily disagree with said Law of Raspberry Jam. My book, 'The Culture Consumers,' mentions it, then spends 14 chapters disputing its contention that 'the wider any culture is spread, the thinner it gets.' " *FD.*)

● **Ehrlich's Rule.** The first rule of intelligent tinkering is to save all the parts.

(Environmentalist Paul Ehrlich, *The Saturday Review,* June 5, 1971.)

● **Ehrman's Corollary to Ginsberg's Theorem.** (1) Things will get worse before they get better. (2) Who said things would get better.

(John Ehrman, Stanford Linear Accelerator Center. *JE.* Of course, you should see *Ginsberg's Theorem.*)

● **Einstein's Other Formula.** If A equals success, then the formula is $A = X + Y + Z$. X is work. Y is play. Z is keep your mouth shut.

(Albert Einstein defining success, news summaries of April 19, 1955, quoted in *Contemporary Quotations,* compiled by J. B. Simpson, Crowell, 1964.)

● **Eliot's Observation.** Nothing is so good as it seems beforehand.

(George Eliot.)

● **Emerson's Insight.** That which we call sin in others is experiment for us.

(Ralph Waldo Emerson.)

● **Engineer's Law, The Old.** The larger the project or job, the less time there is to do it.

(George A. Daher, Philadelphia, to *AO.*)

● **Epstein's Law.** If you think the problem is bad now, just wait until we've solved it.
　　(*U.* From Arthur Kasspé, Ph.D., New York City.)

● **Err's Laws.** See *Murphy's Law(s)*. Err is basically a synonym for Murphy, but those who quote him over the better-known prophet insist he is as real as Murphy. The basis for their argument: (1) his spirit, like Murphy's, is everywhere and (2) Err is human.

● **Eternity Rule.** Nothing is certain except death and taxes. *Bretagna's Corollary*: If anything else is permanent, it is the fact that, given *any* roadway, somewhere upon it there will be someone going slower than you want to go.
　　(The *Eternity Rule* is one of several names currently being given to various close paraphrases of Benjamin Franklin's line, "In this world, nothing is certain but death and taxes." It first appeared in a letter from Franklin to M. Leroy in 1789. The corollary comes from Nicholas Bretagna II, Orlando, Fla.)

● **Ettorre's Observation.** The other line moves faster.
　　(Barbara Ettorre, New York City. This first appeared in *Harper's* in August, 1974, and has become a bona fide hit, showing up on almost every list of laws produced since it was first published. The original was longer than what is now commonly known as *Ettorre's Observation*. The full version: "The Other Line moves faster. This applies to all lines—bank, supermarket, tollbooth, customs, and so on. And don't try to change lines. The Other Line —the one you were in originally—will then move faster." *HW*.)

● **Evans's Law.** Nothing worth a damn is ever done as a matter of principle. (If it is worth doing, it is done because it

is worth doing. If it is not, it's done as a matter of principle.)
(James T. Evans, attorney, Houston.)

● **Evans's Law of Political Perfidy.** When our friends get into power, they aren't our friends anymore.
(M. Stanton Evans, who was until recently the head of the American Conservative Union. *JMcC.*)

● **Evelyn's Rules for Bureaucratic Survival.** (1) A bureaucrat's castle is his desk . . . and parking place. Proceed cautiously when changing either. (2) On the theory that one should never take anything for granted, follow up on everything, but especially those items varying from the norm. The greater the divergence from normal routine and/or the greater the number of offices potentially involved, the better the chance a never-to-be-discovered person will file the problem away in a drawer specifically designed for items requiring a decision. (3) Never say without qualification that your activity has sufficient space, money, staff, etc. (4) Always distrust offices not under your jurisdiction which say that they are there to serve you. "Support" offices in a bureaucracy tend to grow in size and make demands on you out of proportion to their service and in the end require more effort on your part than their service is worth. *Corollary:* Support organizations can always prove success by showing service to someone . . . not necessarily you. (5) Incompetents often hire able assistants.
(Douglas Evelyn, National Portrait Gallery, Washington, D.C.)

● **Everitt's Form of the Second Law of Thermodynamics.** Confusion (entropy) is always increasing in society. Only if someone or something works extremely hard can this confusion be reduced to order in a limited region. Nevertheless, this effort will still result in an increase in the total confusion of society at large.

(Dr. W. L. Everitt, dean emeritus of the College of Engineering at the University of Illinois.)

● **Eve's Discovery.** At a bargain sale, the only suit or dress that you like best and that fits is the one not on sale. *Adam's Corollary*: It's easy to tell when you've got a bargain—it doesn't fit.

(Fred Dyer. *FD*.)

● **Evvie Nef's Law.** There is a solution to every problem; the only difficulty is finding it.

(*Washington Post Potomac,* January, 1972. *JW*.)

● **Expert Advice, The First Law of.** Don't ask the barber whether you need a haircut.

(Science writer-columnist Daniel S. Greenberg first revealed this some years ago in *Saturday Review* and returned to it in late 1977 in his *Washington Post* column. Greenberg attaches the law to ". . . the promotion of a technology by its developers or custodians without any independent check on whether it does what it's supposed to do." He gives several examples, including a chemical shark repellent called Shark Chaser, which the Navy bought in great quantities between World War II and 1974, at which time it was learned that sharks had no aversion to eating Shark Chaser.)

● **Extended Epstein-Heisenberg Principle.** In a research and development orbit, only two of the existing three parameters can be defined simultaneously. The parameters are: task, time and resources ($).

(1) If one knows what the task is, and there is a time limit allowed for the completion of the task, then one cannot guess how much it will cost.

(2) If the time and resources ($) are clearly defined, then it is impossible to know what part of the R&D task will be performed.

(3) If you are given a clearly defined R&D goal and a definite amount of money which has been calculated to be necessary for the completion of the task, one cannot predict if and when the goal will be reached.

(4) If one is lucky enough and can accurately define all three parameters, then what one deals with is not in the realm of R&D.

(From the article "Uncertainty Principle in Research and Development," in *JIR,* January, 1973.)

F

● **Faber's Laws.** (1) If there isn't a law, there will be. (2) The number of errors in any piece of writing rises in proportion to the writer's reliance on secondary sources. (This is also called *The First Law of Historical Research.*)

(Harold Faber. The first was used as the title of his 1968 *New York Times Magazine* article on laws, and the second was created in response to some errors that appeared in the article—i.e. calling Alvin Toffler, Anthony Toffler. [See *Editorial Correction, Law of.*] At the time the article was written, Faber was editorial director of the Book and Education Division of the *Times.*)

● **Falkland's Rule.** When it is not necessary to make a decision, it is necessary not to make a decision.

(Lord Falkland.)

● **Farber's Laws.** (1) Give him an inch and he'll screw you. (2) We're all going down the same road in different directions. (3) Necessity is the mother of strange bedfellows.

(Dave Farber, from a Farberism contest list. *S.T.L.*)

● **Farmer's Law on Junk.** What goes in, comes out. *Corollary 1:* He who sees what comes out, and why, gains wisdom. *Corollary 2:* He who sees only half the problem will be buried in the other half. *Corollary 3:* One man's junk is another's income—and sometimes his priceless antique. *Corollary 4:* Ten thousand years from now, the only story this civilization will tell will be in its junk piles—so observe what is important! *Corollary 5:* Seers and soothsayers read crystal balls to find the future. Less lucky men read junk—with more success. *Corollary 6:* A rose is a rose is a rose, but junk is not junk is not junk. It never is quite what you think it is. *Corollary 7:* Happiness at age ten was finding an empty six pack of returnable Coke bottles. The poor kids these days will never know what they missed, which is why we have a generation gap.

> (Richard N. Farmer, chairperson, International Business School, Indiana University. From his book *Farmer's Law: Junk in a World of Affluence,* Stein & Day Publishers, 1973. One needs to read the whole book to appreciate fully the technique, but the basic law and its corollaries attempt to show you how to read the future, national and international trends, other people's personalities, and competitors' plans—all by reading junk.)

● **Fashion, Law of.** The same dress is indecent 10 years before its time

> daring 1 year before its time
> chic in its time
> dowdy 3 years after its time
> hideous 20 years after its time
> amusing 30 years after its time
> romantic 100 years after its time
> beautiful 150 years after its time

(James Laver. *JW.*)

● **Father Damian Fandal's Rules for [Academic] Deans.** Rule 1—*Hide!!!* Rule 2—*If they find you, lie!!!*

> (Father Damian C. Fandal, O.P., former dean of academic affairs, University of Dallas, Texas.)

● **Fetridge's Law.** Important things that are supposed to happen do not happen, especially when people are looking.

> (Claude Fetridge, an NBC radio engineer in the 1930s. In

1936 he came up with the idea of broadcasting, live of course, the departure of the swallows from their famous roost at Mission San Juan Capistrano. As is well known, the swallows always depart on October 23, St. John's Day. NBC decided that Fetridge's idea was sound and made all due preparations, including sending a crew to the Mission. The sparrows then left a day ahead of schedule.

Fetridge's Law was all but forgotten until H. Allen Smith recalled it in an essay on laws in his classic work *A Short History of Fingers and Other State Papers,* Little Brown, 1963. Smith pointed out that *Fetridge's Law* also has its good points, which are sometimes overlooked. An example from Smith, "In my own case I have often noted that whenever I develop a raging toothache it is a Sunday and the dentists are all on the golf course. Not long ago my toothache hung on through the weekend and Monday morning it was still throbbing and pulsating like a diesel locomotive. I called my dentist and proclaimed an emergency and drove to his office and going up the stairway the ache suddenly vanished altogether.")

● **Fiedler's Forecasting Rules.** (1) *The First Law of Forecasting:* Forecasting is very difficult, especially if it's about the future. (2) *For this reason*: He who lives by the crystal ball soon learns to eat ground glass. (3) *Similarly:* The moment you forecast you know you're going to be wrong, you just don't know when and in which direction. (4) *Nevertheless, always be precise in your forecasts because:* Economists state their GNP growth projections to the nearest tenth of a percentage point to prove they have a sense of humor. (5) *Another basic law:* If the facts don't conform to the theory, they must be disposed of. (6) *If you've always had doubts about the judgment of forecasters, it's quite understandable because:* An economist is a man who would marry Farrah Fawcett-Majors for her money. (7) *By the same* *reasoning, your suspicions about the narrow range of most forecasts are justified:* The herd instinct among forecasters make sheep look like independent thinkers. (8) *Correspondingly:* If a camel is a horse designed by a committee, then a consensus forecast is a camel's behind. (9) *When presenting a forecast:* Give them a number or give them a date, but never both. (10) *When asked to explain your forecast:* Never underestimate the power of a platitude. (11) *And remember Kessel's insight on the value of malarkey:* There must be underinvestment in bulls . . . just look at the rate of return. (12) *Speaking of profits:* Once economists were asked, "If you're so smart, why ain't you rich?" Today they're asked, "Now that you've proved you ain't so smart, how come you got so rich?" (13) *On the use of survey techniques in forecasting:* When you know absolutely nothing about the topic, make your forecast by asking a carefully selected probability sample of 300 others who don't know the answer either. (14) *In a modern economy everything is related to everything else, so:* Forecasters tend to learn less and less about more and more, until in the end they know nothing about everything . . . (15) *The oldest saw about the profession:* If all the economists were laid end to end, they still wouldn't reach a conclusion. (16) *Another oldie:* Ask five economists and you'll get five different explanations (six, if one went to Harvard). (17) *How an economist defines "hard times":* A recession is when my neighbor loses his job. A depression is when I lose my job. A panic is when my wife loses her job. (18) *The boss's supplication:* Lord, please find me a one-armed economist so we won't always hear, "On the other hand . . ." (19) *The forecaster has his own invocation:* Thank God for compensating errors. (20) *Speaking of the Diety:* Most economists think of God as working great multiple regressions in the sky. . . : [Items (21), (22), and (23) are, respectively, *Murphy's Law, O'Toole's Commentary,* and *Finagle's Constant.*] (24) *A forecaster's best defense is a good offense, so:* If you have to forecast, forecast often. (25) *But:* If you're ever right, never let 'em forget it.

(Edgar R. Fiedler, Conference Board economic researcher and vice-president, in the June, 1977, issue of the Conference Board's magazine *Across the Board*.)

● **Fifth Rule.** You have taken yourself too seriously.
(This law comes from Governor du Pont, who uses it to sum up his political laws (see *du Pont's Laws*). He first heard it from NBC's John Chancellor. To quote du Pont:
"A veteran British diplomat had a favorite way to put down a pushy or egotistical junior. The diplomat would call the younger man in for a heart-to-heart talk and quite often at the end of the talk would say, 'Young man, you have broken the Fifth Rule: You have taken yourself too seriously.' That would end the meeting—except that invariably, as the younger man got to the door, he would turn and ask, 'What are the other rules?'
"And the diplomat would smile serenely and answer, 'There *are* no other rules.' ")

Special Section 2

The Finagle File. People had talked about a mysterious scientist named Finagle for many years before November, 1957, when John W. Campbell, Jr., editor of *Astounding Science Fiction,* asked his readers to help him collect and publish Finagle's "famous unwritten laws of science," but after that announcement Finagle became as much a part of scientific lore as Murphy has become to general lore.

The results of Campbell's request were most gratifying; for more than two years the magazine published letters from Finagle's disciples and fans revealing dozens of laws, corollaries, and factors. Here are some of the most important elements of Finaglania:

☐ *Four Basic Rules.*
1. If anything can go wrong in an experiment, it will. 2. No matter what result is anticipated, there is always someone willing to fake it. 3. No matter what the result, there is always someone eager to misinterpret it. 4. No matter what occurs, there is always someone who believes it happened according to his pet theory.

☐ *The Finagle Factor vs. Other Major Factors.*
The Finagle Factor is characterized by changing the Universe to fit the equation.

The Bouguerre Factor changes the equation to fit the Universe.

The Diddle Factor changes things so that the equation and the Universe appear to fit, without requiring any real change in either. This is also known as the "smoothing" or "soothing" factor, mathematically somewhat similar to a damping factor; it has the characteristic of eliminating differences by dropping the subject under discussion to zero importance.

☐ *Finagle's Creed.*
SCIENCE IS TRUTH: DON'T BE MISLED BY FACTS.

☐ *Applied Finaglism.*
The Law of the Too, Too Solid Point. In any collection of data, the figure that is most obviously correct—beyond all need of checking—is the mistake.

> Corollary 1: No one whom you ask for help will see it either. *Corollary 2:* Everyone who stops by with unsought advice will see it immediately.

Finagle's Very Fundamental Finding. If a string has one end, then it has another end.

Finagle's Fifth Rule. Whenever a system becomes completely defined, some damn fool discovers something that either abolishes the system or expands it beyond recognition.

Delay Formula. After adding two weeks to the schedule for unexpected delays, add two more for the unexpected, unexpected delays.

On Corrections. When an error has been detected and corrected, it will be found to have been correct in the first place.

> *Corollary:* After the correction has been found in error, it will be impossible to fit the original quantity back into the equation.

Travel Axiom. He travels fastest who travels alone . . . but he hasn't anything to do when he gets there.

Law of Social Dynamics. If, in the course of several months, only three worthwhile social events take place, they will all fall on the same evening.

☐ *Finagle's Contributions to the Field of Measurement.*
1. Dimensions will be expressed in the least convenient terms, e.g.: Furlongs per (Fortnight)^2 = Measure of Acceleration.
2. Jiffy—the time it takes for light to go one cm in a vacuum.
3. Protozoa are small, and bacteria are small, but viruses are smaller than the both of 'em put together.

☐ *Finagle's Proofs, Household Examples.*
   Any vacuum cleaner would sooner take the nap off a rug than remove white threads from a dark rug.
   No dog will knock a vase over unless it has water in it.

☐ *Finagle's Rules for Scientific Research.*
1. Do Not Believe in Miracles—Rely on Them.
2. Experiments Must Be Reproducible—They Should Fail the Same Way.
3. Always Verify Your Witchcraft.
4. First Draw Your Curves—Then Plot Your Readings.
5. Be Sure to Obtain Meteorological Information Before Leaving on Vacation.

6. A Record of Data is Useful—It Indicates That You've Been Working.
7. Experience Is Directly Proportional to Equipment Ruined.
8. To Study a Subject Best—Understand It Thoroughly Before You Start.
9. In Case of Doubt—Make It Sound Convincing.

☐ *Later Findings.*
In the years since the original information on Finagle appeared in *Astounding Science Fiction,* scores of new laws have been discovered and attributed to Finagle. Here is but one example:
Finagle's Laws of Information.
1. The information you have is not what you want.
2. The information you want is not what you need.
3. The information you need is not what you can obtain.
4. The information you can obtain costs more than you want to pay!

☐ *Friends of Finagle and Examples of Their Laws* (from the original *ASF* letters).
Sprinkle's Law: Things fall at right angles.
Stockmayer's Theorem: If it looks easy, it's tough. If it looks tough, it's damn near impossible.
Deadlock's Law: If the law makers make a compromise, the place where it will be felt most is the taxpayer's pocket. *Corollary:* The compromise will always be more expensive than either of the suggestions it is compromising.

☐ *Aliases, Pseudonyms, and aka's for Dr. Finagle.*
Dr. Henri Bouguerre, Dr. Gwen T. Diddle, Bougar T. Factor, Dr. Finnagle, and Dr. von Nagle.

● **First Thesis.** Everything is nothing. Everything is all. All is one. One is inconceivable, infinite. Therefore it is nothing. Therefore everything is nothing.

Everything is matter. Matter is electricity. Electricity is invisible, intangible. Therefore it is nothing. Therefore everything is nothing.

Atoms are made up of electrons and protons (protons are also nothing). Fifty billion electrons placed side by side in a straight line would stretch across the diameter of the period at the end of this sentence. Protons are heavier but take up less space. Such an idea is incapable of absorption by the human mind.

> (From *The Crowning of Technocracy* by Professor John Lardner and Dr. Thomas Sugrue, 1933, published by "Laboratory of Robert M. McBride & Co., NY.")

● **Fischer's Finding.** Sex is hereditary. If your parents never had it, chances are you won't either.

> (Joseph Fischer, W. Melbourno, Fla. *HW.*)

● **Fishbein's Conclusion.** The tire is only flat on the bottom.

> (*U.* From John L. Shelton, Dallas.)

● **Fitz-Gibbon's Law.** Creativity varies inversely with the number of cooks involved with the broth.

> (Bernice Fitz-Gibbon in *Macy's, Gimbels and Me,* Simon and Schuster, 1967. *FL.*)

● **Flap's Law of the Perversity of Inanimate Objects.** Any inanimate object, regardless of its composition or configuration, may be expected to perform at any time in a totally unexpected manner for reasons that are either totally obscure or completely mysterious.

> (Dr. Fyodor Flap, encountered in Walter Mulé's "Beyomd Murphy's Law." From this Flap builds *Mulé's*

Law. Flap's Law is often identified as *Flagle's Law,* but Flap seems more appropriate.)

● **Flip Wilson's Law.** You can't expect to hit the jackpot if you don't put a few nickles in the machine.
(Wilson on his TV show on October 28, 1971. This was recognized as a universal truth by Thomas Martin.)

● **Forthoffer's Cynical Summary of Barzun's Laws.** See *Barzun's Laws.*

● **Foster's Law.** If you cover a congressional committee on a regular basis, they will report the bill on your day off.
(Herb Foster. According to Foster it was created some years ago when he was at UPI [then UP] and the Senate Appropriations Committee reported out the biggest civil works appropriations up to that point in history. "I knew nothing of the places or projects involved, but had to cover it." Compounded by many later situations involving Foster and others.)

● **Fourth Law of Thermodynamics.** If the probability of success is not almost one, then it is damn near zero.
(David Ellis, from his classic 1957 paper, "Some Precise Formulations on the Alleged Perversity of Nature." *RS.*)

● **Fowler's Law.** In a bureaucracy accomplishment is inversely proportional to the volume of paper used.
(Foster L. Fowler, Jackson, Miss. *AO.*)

● **Frankel's Law.** Whatever happens in government could have happened differently and it usually would have been better if it had. *Corollary:* Once things have happened, no matter how accidentally, they will be regarded as manifestations of an unchangeable Higher Reason.

(Professor Charles Frankel of Columbia University, from his book, *High on Foggy Bottom,* Harper & Row, 1969.)

● **Franklin's Law.** Blessed is he who expects nothing, for he shall not be disappointed.

(Gene Franklin, from an article in *Computers and Automation. JE.*)

● **Franklin's Observation.** He that lives upon Hope dies farting.

(Attributed to Benjamin Franklin, *1974 Expectation of Days. RS.*)

● **Freemon's Rule.** Circumstances can force a generalized incompetent to become competent, at least in a specialized field.

(Frank R. Freemon, of the Department of Neurology, Vanderbilt University School of Medicine, from an article of the same title in the *JIR,* March, 1974. *Freemon's Rule* goes beyond the *Peter Principle* and *Godin's Law* (see each) to explain such individuals as Ulysses S. Grant, Harry S Truman, and Winston Churchill, who all reached a level of incompetence [Truman and Grant failed in business, and Churchill fared badly in politics in the 1930s] and then went on to become competent.)

● **Fried's 23rd Law.** Ideas endure and prosper in inverse proportion to their soundness and validity.

(*U/JW.*)

● **Friendship, The 17th and 18th Rules of.** (17) A friend will refrain from telling you he picked up the same amount of life insurance coverage you did for half the price and his is noncancelable. (18) A friend will let you hold the ladder while he goes up on the roof to install your new TV antenna, which is the biggest son of a bitch you ever saw.

F

62

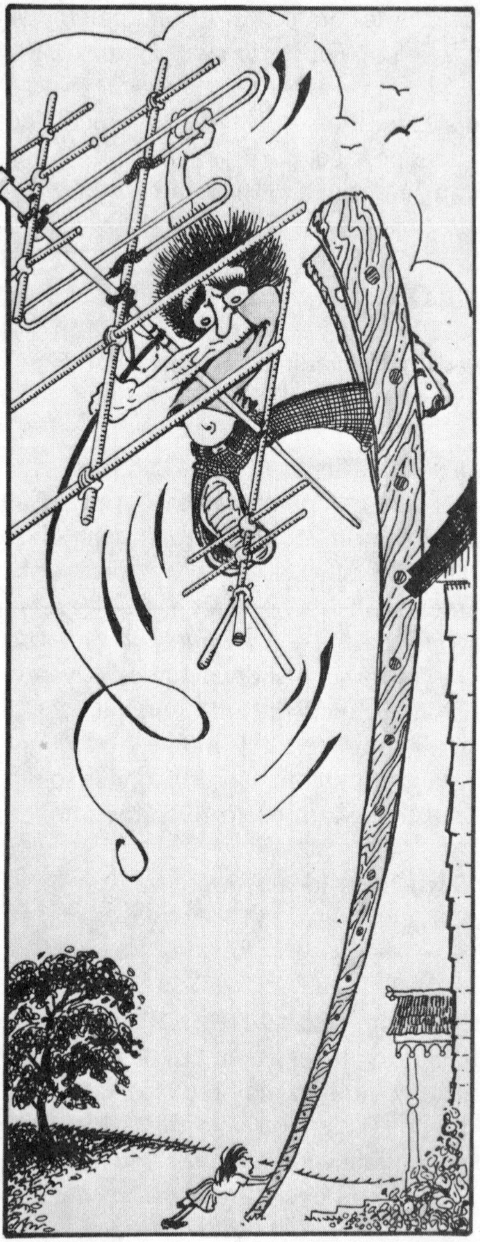

(From "*Esquire*'s 27 Rules of Friendship," which appears in the May, 1977, issue. The items are very clever, but also repetitive. These were picked more or less at random.)

● **Frisbee, The 10 Commandments of the.** (1) The most powerful force in the world is that of a disc straining to land under a car, just beyond reach. (This force is technically termed "car suck.") (2) The higher the quality of a catch or the comment it receives, the greater the probability of a crummy rethrow. (Good catch—bad throw.) (3) One must never precede any maneuver by a comment more predictive than, "Watch this!" (Keep 'em guessing.) (4) The higher the costs of hitting any object, the greater the certainty it will be struck. (Remember—the disc is positive—both cops and old ladies are clearly negative.) (5) The best catches are never seen. ("Did you see that?"—"See what?") (6) The greatest single aid to distance is for the disc to be going in a direction you did not want. (Goes the wrong way = Goes a long way.) (7) The most powerful hex words in the sport are—"I really have this down—watch." (Know it? Blow it!) (8) In any crowd of spectators at least one will suggest that razor blades could be attached to the disc. ("You could maim and kill with that thing.") (9) The greater your need to make a good catch, the greater the probability your partner will deliver his worst throw. (If you can't touch it, you can't trick it.) (10) The single most difficult move with a disc is to put it down. (Just one more.)

> (Dan "The Stork" Roddick, editor of *Frisbee World* and director of the International Frisbee Association. Reprinted with permission from the February, 1975, issue of *Flying Disc World.*)

● **Froben's Law of Publishing.** Never send a letter requesting information to an editor unless you expect to receive a prolix letter in return.

F

64

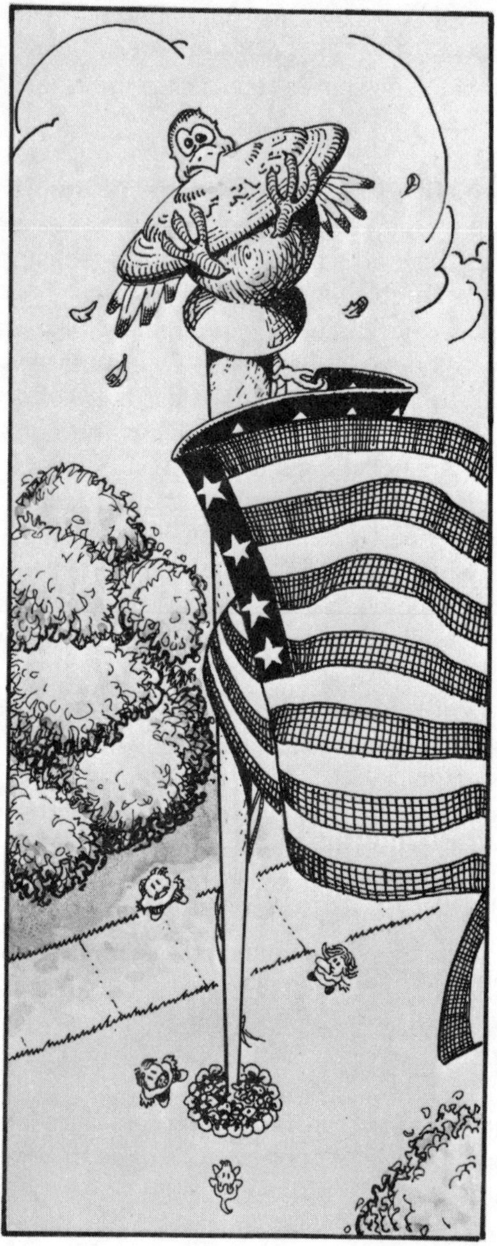

(Froben is the alter ego of Indiana University Press editor Robert Cook.)

● **Froud's Law.** A transistor protected by a fast-acting fuse will protect the fuse by blowing first.
(*U/S.T.L.*)

● **Frustration in the Large, Principle of.** Realization of the expectation total over all events will be as low as possible.
(David Ellis, from "Some Precise Formulations of the Alleged Perversity of Nature," 1957.)

● **Fudd's First Law of Opposition.** If you push something hard enough it will fall over.

● **Fudd's Law of Insertion.** What goes in, must come back out.
(Van Mizzell, Jr., Mobile, Ala.)

● **Fudge Factor.** A physical factor occasionally showing up in experiments as a result of stopping a stopwatch a little early to compensate for reflex error. . . . *Or:* The numerical factor by which experimental results must be multiplied to be in agreement with theory. . . . *Or: Any of a number of other statements used to indicate the conscious addition of a bogus factor or figure.*
(Who was Fudge you ask? Here is the "Fudge" entry from *The Dictionary of Words, Facts and Phrases* by Eliezer Edwards, Chatto & Windus, London, 1901, in its entirety: "*Fudge.* In a 'Collection of some Papers of William Crouch' (8vo. 1712), Crouch, who was a Quaker, says that one Marshall informed him that 'In the year 1664, we were sentenced for banishment to Jamaica by Judges Hyde and Twysden, and our number was 55. We were put on board the ship "Black Eagle," the master's name was *Fudge,* by some called "Lying Fudge." ' Isaac D'Is-

raeli quotes from a pamphlet entitled 'Remarks upon the Navy' (1700), to show that the word originated in a man's name: 'There was, sir, in our time one Captain Fudge, commander of a merchantman, who, upon his return from a voyage, how ill fraught soever his ship was, always brought home his owner a good cargo of lies, so much that now aboard ship the sailors when they hear a great lie told, cry out, "You *fudge* it!" ' ")

● **Fuller's Law of Cosmic Irreversibility.**
$$1 \text{ Pot T} = 1 \text{ Pot P}$$
$$1 \text{ Pot P} \neq 1 \text{ Pot T}$$
(R. Buckminster Fuller.)

● **Funkhouser's Law of the Power of the Press.** The quality of legislation passed to deal with a problem is inversely proportional to the volume of media clamor that brought it on.
(G. Ray Funkhouser, Ph.D., Field Research Corp., San Francisco, *AO*.)

● **Futility Factor.** No experiment is ever a complete failure. It can always serve as a bad example, or the exception that proves the rule (but only if it is the first experiment in the series.)
(Embellished version of *Car[l]son's Consolation*.)

● **Fyffe's Axiom.** The problem-solving process will always break down at the point at which it is possible to determine who caused the problem.
(*U/2p?*)

- **Gadarene Swine Law.** Merely because the group is in formation does not mean that the group is on the right course. (Law derived from the passage in the New Testament in which Christ sent the pigs tumbling into the lake [Mark 5:11–13]. Reported by Robert Cook.)

- **Galbraith's Law of Political Wisdom.** Anyone who says he isn't going to resign, four times, definitely will.

- **Galbraith's Law of Prominence.** Getting on the cover of *Time* guarantees the existence of opposition in the future. (John Kenneth Galbraith. The first from *AO;* the second, *MBC.* See also *Grump's Law.*)

- **Gall's Principles of Systemantics** (1) *The Primal Scenario or Basic Datum of Experience:* Systems in general work poorly or not at all. (2) *The Fundamental Theorem:* New systems generate new problems. (3) *The Law of Conservation of Anergy:* The total amount of energy in the universe is constant.*(4) *Law of Growth:* Systems tend to grow, and as they grow, they encroach. (5) *The Generalized Uncertainty Principle:* Systems display antics.
  (Dr. John Gall, from his book *Systemantics: How Systems Work and Especially How They Fail,* Quadrangle/ The New York Times Book Company, 1977. The laws quoted above are just an abbreviated sampling from a much

*Gall's definition of anergy: "Any state or condition of the Universe, or of any portion of it, that requires the expenditure of human effort or ingenuity to bring it into line with human desires, needs, or pleasures is defined as an ANERGY-STATE."

longer list of axioms and laws revealed and explained in this benchmark book that ranks in importance with *Parkinson's Law* and *The Peter Principle* for anyone trying to understand our modern, technological society. Gall, a professor and practicing physician, has a particular ability to come up with concisely stated truths—e.g., "The dossier is not the person," and "Any large system is going to be operating most of the time in failure mode.")

● **Gallois's Revelation.** If you put tomfoolery into a computer, nothing comes out but tomfoolery. But this tomfoolery, having passed through a very expensive machine, is somehow ennobled, and no one dares to criticize it.

(Pierre Gallois in *Science et Vie,* Paris, reprinted in the *Reader's Digest.*)

● **Gammon's Theory of Bureaucratic Displacement.** In a bureaucratic system an increase in expenditure will be matched by a fall in production. Such systems will act rather like "black holes" in the economic universe, simultaneously sucking in resources and shrinking in terms of "emitted" production. *Or, as restated by Milton Friedman:* In a bureaucratic system, useless work drives out useful work.

(British physician Dr. Max Gammon, on the completion of a five-year study of the British health system. Discussed by Milton Friedman in his November 7, 1977, *Newsweek* column. See also *Parkinson's Law,* of which *Gammon's Theory* is an extension.)

● **Gardening, Laws of.** (1) Other people's tools work only in other people's yards. (2) Fancy gizmos don't work. (3) If nobody uses it, there's a reason. (4) You get the most of what you need the least.

(Jane Bryant Quinn, in her newspaper column syndicated by *The Washington Post,* 1975.)

● **Gardner's Rule of Society.** The society which scorns excellence in plumbing because plumbing is a humble activity and tolerates shoddiness in philosophy because it is an exalted activity will have neither good plumbing nor good philosophy. Neither its pipes nor its theories will hold water.

(John W. Gardner, *Forbes,* "Thought" page, August 1, 1977.)

● **G Constant (or Godin's Law).** Generalizedness of incompetence is directly proportional to highestness in hierarchy. (Guy Godin, from an article with the same title in *JIR,* March, 1972. Godin has found an exception to the *Peter Principle* because he argues that some people are incompetent before they begin to rise. Peter argues that they rise to their level of incompetence. See also *Freemon's Rule.*)

● **Geanangel's Law.** If you want to make an enemy, do someone a favor.
(Charles L. Geanangel, teacher, Winter Haven, Fla. *JMcC.*)

● **Gell-Mann's Dictum.** Whatever isn't forbidden is required. *Corollary:* If there's no reason why something shouldn't exist, then it must exist.
(Murray Gell-Mann. *JW.*)

● **Germond's Law.** When a group of newsmen go out to dinner together, the bill is to be divided evenly among them, regardless of what each one eats and drinks.
(Newsman-columnist Jack Germond. See also *Weaver's Law,* of which Germond's is a corollary. *AO.*)

● **Gerrold's Laws of Infernal Dynamics.** (1) An object in motion will always be headed in the wrong direction. (2) An object at rest will always be in the wrong place. (3) The energy required to change either one of these states will always be more than you wish to expend, but never so much as to make the task totally impossible.
(David Gerrold, writer and columnist for *Starlog* magazine. See *Short's Quotations,* which are also his.)

● **Getty's Reminder.** The meek shall inherit the earth, but *not* its mineral rights.

(J. Paul Getty, quoted by Earl Wilson, among others.)

● **Gilb's Laws of Reliability.** (1) Computers are unreliable, but humans are even more unreliable. *Corollary:* At the source of every error which is blamed on the computer you will find at least two human errors, including the error of blaming it on the computer. (2) Any system which depends on human reliability is unreliable. (3) The only difference between the fool and the criminal who attacks a system is that the fool attacks unpredict-ably and on a broader front. (4) A system tends to grow in terms of complexity rather than of simplification, until the resulting unreliability becomes intolerable. (5) Self-checking systems tend to have a complexity in proportion to the inherent unreliability of the system in which they are used. (6) The error-detection and correction capabilities of any system will serve as the key to understanding the type of errors which they cannot handle. (7) Undetectable errors are infinite in variety, in contrast to detecta-ble errors, which by definition are limited. (8) All real programs contain errors until proved otherwise—which is impossible. (9) Investment in reliability will increase until it exceeds the probable cost of errors, or somebody insists on getting some useful work done.

(Tom Gilb, "The Laws of Unreliability," *Datamation,* March, 1975. *JE.*)

● **Gilmer's Law of Political Leadership.** Look over your shoulder now and then to be sure someone's following you.

(Uttered by Virginia's State Treasurer Henry Gilmer some 30 years ago and recently quoted in a column by James J. Kilpatrick.)

● **Ginsberg's Theorem.** (1) You can't win. (2) You can't break even. (3) You can't even quit the game.

(*U/S.T.L.* See *Ehrman's Corollary.*)

● **Glasow's Law.** There's something wrong if you're always right.

(Arnold Glasow, quoted on *Forbes's* "Thought" page, March 15, 1977.)

● **Golden Principle.** Nothing will be attempted if all possible objections must first be overcome.

(Posted in Department of Labor. *TO'B.*)

● **Golden Rule of the Arts and Sciences, The (GRASS).** Whoever has the gold makes the rules.

(This important and oft-quoted rule was announced in the *Journal of Irreproducible Results* in 1975 by O. W. Knewittoo—either a pseudonym or an Eskimo scientist.)

● **Gold's Law. [V.]** The candidate who is expected to do well because of experience and reputation (Douglas, Nixon) must do *better* than well, while the candidate expected to fare poorly (Lincoln, Kennedy) can put points on the media board simply by surviving.

(Vic Gold, in *P.R. as in President,* Doubleday, 1977.)

● **Gold's Law. [W.]** A column about errors will contain errors.

(Popular *Washington Post* columnist Bill Gold, who announced this law in May, 1978, after he had done a column on glitches that get into print—i.e., the "not" which disappears from "not guilty." Before it went into print Gold was able to find and rid the column of three errors and his copy editor was able to find two more. After all of this (more than 20 careful readings) a just-for-good-measure final reading was made by still another editor and it was put into type. When the first edition of the paper came out, the three segments of the column [or legs] had been pasted up wrong so that the last section was in the middle and the middle at the end.)

● **Goldwyn's Law of Contracts.** A verbal contract isn't worth the paper it's written on.
(Samuel Goldwyn. *Co.*)

● **Golub's Laws of Computerdom.** (1) Fuzzy project objectives are used to avoid the embarrassment of estimating the corresponding costs. (2) A carelessly planned project takes three times longer to complete than expected; a carefully planned project will take only twice as long. (3) The effort required to correct course increases geometrically with time. (4) Project teams detest weekly progress reporting because it so vividly manifests their lack of progress.
(*U/JE.*)

● **Goodfader's Law.** Under any system a few sharpies will beat the rest of us.
(Al Goodfader, Washington, D.C. *AO.*)

● **Gordon's First Law.** If a research project is not worth doing at all, it is not worth doing well.
(*U/RS.*)

● **Goulden's Axiom of the Bouncing Can (ABC).** If you drop a full can of beer, and remember to rap the top sharply with your knuckle prior to opening, the ensuing gush of foam will be between 89 and 94 percent of the volume that would splatter you if you didn't do a damned thing and went ahead and pulled the top immediately.

● **Goulden's Law of Jury Watching.** If a jury in a criminal trial stays out for more than twenty-four hours, it is certain to vote acquittal, save in those instances where it votes guilty.

(Joseph C. Goulden, writer, developed the second law during twenty-seven months of intensive research as a courts reporter for *The Dallas News.*)

● **Graditor's Laws.** (1) If it can break, it will, but only after the warranty expires. (2) A necessary item only goes on sale after you have purchased it at the regular price.
(Sherry Graditor, Skokie, Ill.)

● **Grandma Soderquist's Conclusion.** A chicken doesn't stop scratching just because the worms are scarce.
(Letter from John Peers of Logical Machine Corp., thanking contributors for laws for that company's law collection.)

● **Gray's Law of Bilateral Asymmetry in Networks.** Information flows efficiently through organizations, except that bad news encounters high impedance in flowing upward.
(Paul Gray to Robert Machol for his *POR* series. Gray also told Machol, ". . . people at the top make decisions as though times were good when people at the bottom know that the organization is collapsing.")

● **Gray's Law of Programming.** $n+1$ trivial tasks are expected to be accomplished in the same time as n trivial tasks.
(*U/S.T.L.* See *Logg's Rebuttal to Gray's Law of Programming.*)

● **Greener's Law.** Never argue with a man who buys ink by the barrel.
(Bill Greener. *AO.*)

● **Greenberg's First Law of Influence.** Usefulness is inversely proportional to reputation for being useful.
(Daniel S. Greenberg, in a column entitled "Debunking

the UTK [Useful to Know] Myth," *The Washington Post,*
October 25, 1977. He attacks the conventional wisdom
that says there are people who are useful to know in the
sense that they possess inordinate influence. He makes
many points in favor of his law, including this one: "What
must be noted about the many fallen political celebrities
of recent years is that salvation eluded them, though they
knew all the people in Washington who are useful to
know.")

● **Gresham's Law.** Bad money drives out good.
(Sir Thomas Gresham discovered this law in the sixteenth
century. It has been generalized, restated, and redirected
to a number of fields, so it appears in many forms, including the currently popular version that says, "Trivial matters are handled promptly; important matters are never
solved." An example of a specialized application is
"Gresham's TV Law," which appeared in a January 2,
1977, article by Frank Mankiewicz in *The Washington
Post:* "In a Medium in which a News Piece takes a minute and an 'In-Depth' Piece takes two minutes, the Simple
will drive out the Complex.")

● **Groebe's Thought on Memory.** If you can't remember
it, it couldn't have been important.
(Larry Groebe John L. Shelton, Dallas.)

● **Grosch's Law.** Computing power increases as the square
of the cost. If you want to do it twice as cheaply, you have to
do it four times as fast.
(Herb Grosch, editor, *Computerworld. S.T.L.*)

● **Gross's Law.** When two people meet to decide how to
spend a third person's money, fraud will result.
(Herman Gross, Great Neck, N.Y. *AO.*)

● **Grump's Law.** If both Alsops say it's true, it can't be so. (From an undated, unauthenticated paper entitled "Great Days for Grump's Law" by John Kenneth Galbraith. He insists that this law is invaluable in American political forecasting but adds, "As a man of more than average caution, I have never felt absolutely secure until Evans and Novak have spoken." The paper appears to have been written in 1972.)

● **Gummidge's Law.** The amount of expertise varies in inverse proportion to the number of statements understood by the general public.

(From an essay in *Time,* December 30, 1966, entitled "Right You Are If You Say You Are—Obscurely." The item opens with a scene at Instant College, where a student is being briefed by key faculty members on the importance of learning jargon on the way to becoming an Expert. Dr. Gummidge, professor of sociology, tells the student, "Remember Gummidge's Law and you will never be Found Out." Gummidge illustrates by telling the student how he would tell the student's mother that he was a lazy, good-for-nothing: "The student in question is performing minimally for his peer group and is an emerging underachiever.")

● **Gumperson's Law.** The probability of anything happening is in inverse ratio to its desirability.

(This very important law first appeared in the November, 1957, issue of *Changing Times* and was credited to Dr. R. F. Gumperson [although we have subsequently learned that the real author is John W. Hazard, now the magazine's executive editor]. The law was announced in conjunction with a long-forgotten article on firewood, to account for a phenomenon known to anyone who has ever lit fires, to wit: ". . . that you can throw a burnt match out the window of your car and start a forest fire while you can use two boxes of matches and a whole edition of the Sunday paper without being able to start a fire under the dry logs in your fireplace."

Gumperson began serious work in 1938 on the *Farmers' Almanac* phenomenon [by which that esteemed annual always does a better job predicting the weather than the official weather bureau] and during World War II went on to develop the procedure for the armed forces ". . . whereby the more a recruit knew about a given subject, the better chance he had of receiving an assignment involving some other subject."

Some of the many real-life examples he was able to derive from his law and his pioneering work as a divicist:*

✪ That after a raise in salary you will have less money at the end of each month than you had before.

✪ That children have more energy after a hard day of play than they do after a good night's sleep.

✪ That the person who buys the most raffle tickets has the least chance of winning.

✪ That good parking places are always on the other side of the street.

It was further reported that Gumperson met with an untimely death in 1947 while walking down the highway. He was obeying the proper rule of walking on the left facing traffic when he was hit from behind by a Hillman-Minx driven by an Englishman hugging the left.

Over the years Gumperson has picked up many disciples, including the late H. Allen Smith, who wrote that he felt that the law was written just for him. One of Smith's many examples: "I dislike going to the garage with a rattle

---

*One skilled in divicism. Divicism is the science of making predictions according to the law of diverges. A diverge is the opposite of an average.

in my car, because the moment the mechanic begins his inspection, that rattle will vanish.'')

● **Gumperson's Proof.** The most undesirable things are the most certain (e.g., death and taxes).

(From Martin S. Kottmeyer, Carlyle, Illinois.)

● **Guthman's Law of Media.** Thirty seconds on the evening news is worth a front page headline in every newspaper in the world.

(Edwin Guthman. *MBC's Laws of Politics.*)

- **Hacker's Law.** The belief that enhanced understanding will necessarily stir a nation or an organization to action is one of mankind's oldest illusions.

- **Hacker's Law of Personnel.** It is never clear just how many hands—or minds—are needed to carry out a particular process. Nevertheless, anyone having supervisory responsibility for the completion of the task will invariably protest that his staff is too small for the assignment.

  (Andrew Hacker, from *The End of the American Dream,* Atheneum, 1970. The *Law of Personnel* has been revised on various lists and is sometimes written as: "Anyone having supervisory responsibility for the completion of a task will invariably protest that more resources are needed.")

- **Hagerty's Law.** If you lose your temper at a newspaper columnist, he'll get rich or famous or both.

  (James C. Hagerty, President Eisenhower's press secretary, who discovered it after blowing his top over a column by humorist Art Buchwald. *FL.* For other press-secretary laws, see *Nessen's Law, Powell's Laws, Ross's Law,* and *Salinger's Law.*)

- **Halberstam's Law of Survival.** Always stay in with the outs.

  (David Halberstam. *MBC*'s *Laws of Politics.*)

- **Haldane's Law.** The universe is not only stranger than we imagine, it is stranger than we *can* imagine.

  (J. B. S. Haldane, British geneticist and Marxist. *JW.*)

● **Hale's Rule.** The sumptuousness of a company's annual report is in inverse proportion to its profitability that year.
(Irving Hale, the Sarvis Group Inc., Denver. *AO.*)

● **Hall's Law.** There is a statistical correlation between the number of initials in an Englishman's name and his social class (the upper class having significantly more than three names, while members of the lower class average 2.6).
(*U//W.*)

● **Halpern's Observation.** That tendency to err that programmers have been noticed to share with other human beings has often been treated as if it were an awkwardness attendant upon programming's adolescence, which like acne would disappear with the craft's coming of age. It has proved otherwise.
(Mark Halpern. *JE.*)

● **Harden's Law. [F.]** Every time you come up with a terrific idea, you find that someone else thought of it first.
(Frank Harden, radio personality, Washington, D.C. *JW.*)

● **Hardin's Law. [G.]** You can never do merely one thing. (Biologist Garrett Hardin. It applies to any complex system and tells us that even when an action has its intended effect, it also has other, unintended, effects. An editorial in the February, 1974, *Fortune* said, in part, "If a prize were to be awarded for the most illuminating single sentence authored in the past ten years, one of the candidates would surely be Hardin's Law . . ." *Fortune* said examples were common: e.g., New York City's off-track betting system had its intended effect of weaning waging away from illegal bookies, but it also had the unintended effect of creating a new clientele of horseplayers.)

● **Harris's Law.** Any philosophy that can be put "in a nutshell" belongs there.

● **Harris's Restaurant Paradox.** One of the greatest unsolved riddles of restaurant eating is that the customer usually gets faster service when the restaurant is crowded than when it is half empty; it seems that the less that the staff has to do, the slower they do it.

> (Sydney J. Harris, the first from his book *Leaving the Surface,* 1968, and the second from *On the Contrary,* 1964, both published by Houghton Mifflin.)

● **Hartig's How Is Good Old Bill? We're Divorced Law.** If there is a wrong thing to say, one will.

> (Betty Hartig, "the Nantucket Kitelady.")

● **Hartig's Sleeve in the Cup, Thumb in the Butter Law.** When one is trying to be elegant and sophisticated, one won't.

● **Hartley's Law.** You can lead a horse to water, but if you can get him to float on his back you've got something.

> (Let Conrad Schneiker explain how he acquired this law: "Hartley was a University of Arizona student who wandered into my office looking lost, circa 1974." *S.T.L.*)

● **Hartman's Automotive Laws.** (1) Nothing minor ever happens to a car on the weekend. (2) Nothing minor ever happens to a car on a trip. (3) Nothing minor ever happens to a car.

> (Charles D. Hartman, Belleair, Fla.)

● **Hart's Law of Observation.** In a country as big as the United States, you can find fifty examples of anything.

> (*U.* Jeffery F. Chamberlain letter to *Verbatim.*)

● **Harvard Law.** Under the most rigorously controlled conditions of pressure, temperature, volume, humidity, and other variables, the organism will do as it damn well pleases.
(*U/Co.*)

● **Hein's Law.** Problems worthy of attack prove their worth by hitting back.
(Piet Hein, from a group of "Quips" in *Journal of Irreproducible Results*, March, 1971.)

● **Heller's Myths of Management.** The first myth of management is that it exists. The second myth of management is that success equals skill.
(Robert Heller, *The Great Executive Dream*, Delacorte, 1972. *JE*. See *Johnson's Corollary* to *Heller's Law*.)

● **Herblock's Law.** If it's good they'll stop making it.
(Conceived by the famous political cartoonist after they stopped making a particular kind of carbon drawing stick that he liked best. Reported on by Sydney J. Harris in his December 28, 1977, syndicated column, "Modern Way: If It's Good, Scrap It." *FD*.)

● **Herrnstein's Law.** The attention paid to an instructor is a constant regardless of the size of the class. Thus as class size swells, the amount of attention paid per student drops in direct ratio.
(Psychologist Richard J. Herrnstein. *AO*.)

● **Hersh's Law.** Biochemistry expands so as to fill the space and time available for its completion and publication.
(R. T. Hersh, in a 1962 *American Scientist* article, "Parkinson's Law, the Squid and pU.")

● **Hildebrand's Law.** The quality of a department is inversely proportional to the number of courses it lists in its catalogue.

(Professor Joel Hildebrand, University of California at Berkeley.)

● **Historian's Rule.** Any event, once it has occurred, can be made to appear inevitable by a competent historian.
(Lee Simonson, from Herbert V. Prochow's *The Public Speaker's Treasure Chest,* Harper & Row, 1977.)

● **Hoare's Law of Large Programs.** Inside every large program is a small program struggling to get out.
(Tony Hoare, computer scientist. *S.T.L.*)

● **Hogg's (Murphy's) Law of Station Wagons.** The amount of junk carried is in direct proportion to the amount of space available. *Baggage Corollary:* If you go on a trip taking two bags with you, one containing everything you need for the trip and the other containing absolutely nothing, the second bag will be completely filled with junk acquired on the trip when you return.
(Tony Hogg, in an *Esquire* article, "The Right Way to Buy a New Small Car," February, 1975.)

● **Hollywood's Iron Law.** Nothing succeeds like failure.
(Discussed and reapplied by Sidney Zion in his article "Hollywood's Iron Law Comes to Washington," *New York,* January 24, 1977. As Zion explains, ". . . if a genius lost a few million on a picture, he was immediately installed in a fancier office with a better title and a bigger budget. . . . Only after nine straight flops was he eligible to become head of the studio.")

● **Horner's Five-Thumb Postulate.** Experience varies directly with equipment ruined.
(Presumably, Little Jack Horner. *A/C.*)

Special Section 3

HOW TO . . .

△ *Kill an Enterprise.*

(1) Do not go to meetings.

(2) If you go, arrive late.

(3) Criticize the work of the organizers and members.

(4) Get mad if you are not a member of the committee, but if you are, make no suggestions.

(5) If the chair asks your opinion on a subject, say you have none. After the meeting say you have learned nothing, or tell everyone what should have happened.

(6) Don't do what has to be done yourself, but when the members roll up their sleeves and do their very best, complain that the group is run by a bunch of ego-trippers.

(7) Pay your dues as late as possible.

(8) Never think of introducing new members.

(9) Complain that nothing is ever published which interests you but never offer to write an article, make a suggestion, or find a writer.

(10) And if the enterprise dies, say you saw it coming ages before.

> (Jean-Charles Terrassier, founder of the French Society for Gifted Children, who listed these suggestions in *Quipos,* the international French journal.)

△ *Make Yourself Miserable.*

(1) Forget the good things in life and concentrate on the bad.

(2) Put an excessive value on money.

(3) Think that you are indispensable to your job, your community, and your friends.

(4) Think that you are overburdened with work and that people tend to take advantage of you.

(5) Think that you are exceptional and entitled to special privileges.

(6) Think that you can control your nervous system by sheer willpower.

(7) Forget the feelings and rights of other people.

(8) Cultivate a consistently pessimistic outlook.

(9) Never overlook a slight or forget a grudge.

(10) And don't forget to feel sorry for yourself.
   (U/TO'B.)

△ *Tell Republicans from Democrats.*

•Democrats buy most of the books that have been banned somewhere. Republicans form censorship committees and read them as a group.

•Republicans consume three-fourths of all the rutabaga produced in this country. The remainder is thrown out.

•Republicans usually wear hats and almost always clean their paint brushes.

•Democrats give their worn-out clothes to those less fortunate. Republicans wear theirs.

•Republicans employ exterminators. Democrats step on the bugs.

•Democrats name their children after currently popular sports figures, politicians, and entertainers. Republican children are named after their parents or grandparents, according to where the money is.

•Democrats keep trying to cut down on smoking but are not successful. Neither are Republicans.

•Republicans tend to keep their shades drawn, although there is seldom any reason why they should. Democrats ought to, but don't.

•Republicans study the financial pages of the newspaper. Democrats put them in the bottom of the bird cage.

•Most of the stuff alongside the road has been thrown out of car windows by Democrats.

•Republicans raise dahlias, Dalmatians, and eyebrows. Democrats raise Airedales, kids, and taxes.

•Democrats eat the fish they catch. Republicans hang them on the wall.

•Republican boys date Democratic girls. They plan to marry Republican girls, but feel they're entitled to a little fun first.

•Democrats make up plans and then do something else. Republicans follow the plans their grandfathers made.

•Republicans sleep in twin beds—some even in separate rooms. That is why there are more Democrats.

(Document submitted and published in the *Congressional Record,* October 1, 1974, by Representative Craig Hosmer [R-Cal.]. Hosmer said that the author chose to remain anonymous.)

△ *Test Yourself for Paranoia.*

You know you've got it when you can't think of anything that's your fault.

(Robert Hutchins.)

△ *Work It So That You Get Your Face on a Postage Stamp.*

We cannot put the face of a person on a stamp unless said person is deceased. My suggestion, therefore, is that you drop dead.

(James Edward Day, postmaster general, in a letter dictated but not mailed to a man who wanted his likeness on a postage stamp. *The New York Times,* March 7, 1962.)

● **Howe's Law.** Every man has a scheme that will not work. (*U/S.T.L.*)

● **Hull's Warning.** Never insult an alligator until after you have crossed the river.

(Cordell Hull.)

● **Human Rights Articles, A Sampling of Proposed.** *Article I:* All men are born naked. *Article VIII:* All men have the right to wait in line. *Article XV:* Each person has the right to take part in the management of public affairs in his country, provided he has prior experience, a will to succeed, a college degree, influential parents, good looks, a résumé, two 3×4 snapshots, and a good tax record. *Article XVI:* Each person has the right to take the subway. *Article XXI:* Everyone has the right, without exception, to equal pay for equal work. Except women.

(Carlos Eduardo Novaes, columnist for *Jornal do Brasil* of Rio, from a much larger collection that appeared in *Atlas.* It was written after the Organization of American States [OAS] was unable to get anywhere in its 1977 debate on human rights. Novaes created a Universal Declaration on Human Rights that he felt that most members of the OAS and UN could live with.)

● **IBM Pollyanna Principle.** Machines should work. People should think.

> (IBM motto, so titled on various computer-oriented lists. *S.T.L., JE,* etc.)

● **Idea Formula.** One man's brain plus one other will produce about one half as many ideas as one man would have produced alone. These two plus two more will produce half again as many ideas. These four plus four more begin to represent a creative meeting, and the ratio changes to one quarter as many. . . .

> (Anthony Chevins, vice-president of Cunningham and Walsh, in an *Advertising Age* article entitled "The Positive Power of Lonethink," April 27, 1959. J.B. Simpson's *Contemporary Quotations,* Crowell, 1964.)

● **Imhoff's Law.** The organization of any bureaucracy is very much like a septic tank—the really big chunks always rise to the top.

> (This first appeared in Thomas L. Martin's *Malice in Blunderland,* McGraw-Hill, 1971, with the following footnote: "Professor John Imhoff, Head of Industrial Engineering, University of Arkansas. A distant cousin, Karl Imhoff, invented the Imhoff Septic Tank of international fame.)

● **Index of Development.** The degree of a country's development is measured by the ratio of the price of an automobile to that of the cost of a haircut. The lower the ratio, the higher the degree of development.

(Samuel Devons, professor of physics, Columbia University, from Charles P. Issawi's *Issawi's Laws of Social Motion*.)

● **Inertia, Law of.** Given enough time, what you put off doing today will eventually get done by itself.
(G. Gestra, Oregon.)

● **Instant Status, Merrill's Rules and Maxims of.** (1) The early bird catches the worm as a rule, but the guy who comes along later may be having lobster Newburg and crêpes suzette. (2) Genuine status is a rare and precious jewel, and also rather easy to simulate. (3) In a democracy you can be respected though poor, but don't count on it. (4) Society heaps honors on the unique, creative personality, but not until he has been dead for fifty years. (5) Money is not the measure of a man, but it will do quite nicely if you don't have any other yardstick handy. (6) If at first you don't succeed, you must be doing something wrong. (7) Everybody believes in rugged individualism, but you'll do better by pleasing the boss. (8) To those who doubt the importance of careful mate selection, remember how Adam wrecked a promising career. (9) It is nice to be content in a little house by the side of the road, but a split-level in suburbia is a lot more comfortable . . .

> (Charles Merrill Smith, from his book *Instant Status, or How to Become a Pillar of the Upper Middle Class*, Doubleday, 1972. These ten rules and maxims come from a longer list of fifteen. All but one of the remaining items are amplifications of the status theme, save for number fourteen, which states, "When God created two sexes, he may have been overdoing it.")

● **Institutional Food, Laws of.** (1) Everything is cold except what should be. (2) Everything, including the cornflakes, is greasy.

(*U.* Part of a collection originating at East Russell Hall, University of Georgia, Athens.)

● **Inverse Appreciation, Law of.** The less there is between you and the environment, the more you appreciate the environment.

(*U//JW.*)

● **Iron Law of Distribution.** Them what has—gets.

(*Co.*)

● **Issawi's Laws of Social Motion** (A Sampling). *Aggression:* At any given moment, a society contains a certain amount of accumulated (stock, ΣA) and accruing (flow, flow, $\Delta A/\Delta T$) aggressiveness. If more than twenty-one years elapse without this aggressiveness being directed outward, in a popular war against other countries, it turns inward, in social unrest, civil disturbances, and political disruption. *Committo-Dynamics, First Law of: Comitas comitatum, omnia comitas. Committo-Dynamics, Second Law of:* The less you enjoy serving on committees, the more likely you are to be pressed to do so. (Explanation: If you do not like committees, you keep quiet, nod your head, and look wise while thinking of something else and thereby acquire the reputation of being a judicious and cooperative colleague; if you enjoy committees, you talk a lot, make many suggestions and are regarded by the other members as a nuisance. *Conservation of Evil, Law of:* The total amount of evil in any system remains constant. Hence any diminution in one direction—for instance a reduction in poverty or unemployment—is accompanied by an increase in another, e.g., crime or air pollution. *Consumption Patterns:* Other people's patterns of expenditure and consumption are highly irrational and slightly immoral. *Cynics:* Cynics are right nine times out of ten; what undoes them is their belief that they are right ten times out of ten. *A Depressing Thought:* One cannot make an omelette without breaking eggs—but it is amazing how many eggs one can break without making a decent omelette. *Dogmatism:* When we call others dogmatic, what we really object to is their holding dogmas that are different from our own. *Factor of Error:* Experts in advanced countries underestimate by a factor of 2 to 4 the ability of people in underdeveloped countries to do anything technical. (Examples: Japanese on warplanes, Russians on the bomb, Iranians on refineries . . . etc.) *Near and Distant Neighbors:* All countries hate their immediate neighbors and like the next but one. (For example, the Poles hate the Germans, Russians, Czechs, and Lithuanians, and they like the French, Hungarians, Italians, and Latvians.) *Operational Definition of Development:* In an underdeveloped country, when you are absent, your job is taken away from you; in a developed country a new one is piled on you. *Path of Progress:* A shortcut is the longest distance between two points. *Petroleum, Law of:* (formulated circa 1951) Where there are Muslims, there is oil; the converse is not true. *Social Science Theories:* By the time a social science theory is formulated in such a way that it can be tested, changing circumstances have already made it obsolete.

(Professor Charles P. Issawi, Princeton economist and author, from his 1973 book *Issawi's Laws of Social Motion,* Hawthorne Books. Issawi uses the book to attempt for social science what Darwin did for biology and Newton did for physics—to state universal laws. He has succeeded, right down to his "Last Words of Advice," which are: "If you pay your taxes and don't get into debt and go to bed early and never answer the telephone—no harm can befall you.")

J

● **Jacoby's Law.** The more intelligent and competent a woman is in her adult life, the less likely she is to have received an adequate amount of romantic attention in adolescence.

> (Susan Jacoby in *The New York Times.* "If a girl was smart," she goes on to explain, "and if she attended an American high school between 1930 and 1965, chances are that no one paid attention to anything but her brains unless she took the utmost care to conceal them.")

● **Jacquin's Postulate on Democratic Governments.** No man's life, liberty, or property are safe while the legislature is in session.

> (*U/S.T.L.*)

● **Jake's Law.** Anything hit with a big enough hammer will fall apart.

> (Robert A. "Jake" Jackson, Socorro, N.M.)

● **Jaroslovsky's Law.** The distance you have to park from your apartment increases in proportion to the weight of packages you are carrying.

> (*U/AO.*)

● **Jay's Laws of Leadership.** (1) Changing things is central to leadership, and changing them before anyone else is creativeness. (2) To build something that endures, it is of the greatest importance to have a long tenure in office—to rule for many years. You can achieve a quick success in a year or two, but nearly all of the great tycoons have continued their building much longer.

(Antony Jay, from *Management and Machiavelli,* Holt, Rinehart and Winston, 1967.)

● **Jinny's Law.** There is no such thing as a short beer. (As in, "I'm going to stop off at Joe's for a short beer before I meet you.")
(Virginia W. Smith. *MLS.*)

● **John Adams's Law of Erosion.** Once the erosion of power begins, it has a momentum all its own.
(From *MBC*'s *Laws of Politics.*)

● **John Cameron's Law.** No matter how many times you've had it, if it's offered, take it, because it'll never be quite the same again.

● **John's Axiom.** When your opponent is down, kick him.

● **John's Collateral Corollary.** In order to get a loan you must first prove you don't need it.
(All John Cameron, who, says Conrad Schneiker, is "a Kansas farmer and friend of 'Big' Peggy.")

● **Johnson's Corollary to Heller's Law.** Nobody really knows what is going on anywhere within your organization.
(*U/S.T.L.*)

● **Johnson's First Law of Auto Repair.** Any tool dropped while repairing an automobile will roll under the car to the vehicle's exact geographic center.
(*U/S.T.L.* Similar to *Anthony's Law of the Workshop.*)

● **Johnson's "Prior" Laws of Politics.** (1) Pay your dues. (2) Attend the meetings.
(Lyndon B. Johnson. The "prior" in the title refers to the

fact that they precede *Dirksen's Laws of Politics* and must be understood "prior" to understanding Dirksen's Laws. Harry N. D. Fisher to *AO.*)

● **Jones's Law.** The man who can smile when things go wrong has thought of someone he can blame it on.
(*Co.* This item appears in virtually every collection of laws, yet there is no clue as to who Jones is. Nor do we know the identity of the Jones of the next law. See also *Tom Jones's First Law.*)

● **Jones's Principle.** Needs are a function of what other people have.
(*U//JW.*)

● **Journalist's Adage.** Never assume anything except a 4¼ percent mortgage.
(Dave Kindred, from his "This Morning" column in *The Washington Post,* January 14, 1978.)

● **Joyce's Law of Bathroom Hooks.** A bathroom hook will be loaded to capacity immediately upon becoming available.
(John Joyce, Waldie and Briggs Inc., Chicago. *AO.* According to Joyce there is more to this law than immediately meets the eye, as it ". . . applies to freeways, closets, playgrounds, downtown hotels, taxis, parking lots, bookcases, wallets, purses, pockets, pipe racks, basement shelves, and so on. The list is endless." However, he is the first to concede that further research is called for. As he told Otten in a note, "The ultimate test of the law, which I have been postponing, would be to array hooks in a continuous strip around the bathroom to see if the towels, bathrobes, etc., actually meet in the middle of the room preventing opening of the door and entry of would-be bathers.")

K

● **Kafka's Law.** In the fight between you and the world, back the world.

(Franz Kafka. RS's *1974 Expectation of Days.*)

● **Kamin's Seventh Law.** Politicians will always inflate when given the opportunity.

(Identified by Conrad Schneiker as an economist from Ventura, California.)

● **Kaplan's Law of the Instrument.** Give a small boy a hammer and he will find that everything he encounters needs pounding.

(Abraham Kaplan. *S.T.L.*)

● **Katz's Maxims.** (1) Where are the calculations that go with the calculated risk? (2) Inventing is easy for staff outfits. Stating a problem is much harder. Instead of stating problems, people like to pass out half-accurate statements together with half-available solutions which they can't finish and which they want you to finish. (3) Every organization is self-perpetuating. Don't ever ask an outfit to justify itself, or you'll be covered with facts, figures, and fancy. The criterion should rather be, "What will happen if the outfit stops doing what it's doing?" The value of an organization is easier determined this way. (4) Try to find out who's doing the work, not who's writing about it, controlling it, or summarizing it. (5) Watch out for formal briefings, they often produce an avalanche. (Definition: A high-level snow job of massive and overwhelming proportions.) (6) The difficulty of the coordination task often blinds one to the fact that a fully coordinated piece of paper is not supposed to be either the major or the final product of the organization, but it often turns out that way. (7) Most organizations can't hold more than one idea at a time . . . Thus complementary ideas are always regarded as competitive. Further, like a quantized pendulum, an organization can jump from one extreme to the other, without ever going through the middle. (8) Try to find the real tense of the report you are reading: Was it done, is it being done, or is it something to be done? Reports are now written in four tenses: past tense, present tense, future tense, and pretense. Watch for novel uses of CONGRAM (CONtractor GRAMmar), defined by the imperfect past, the insufficient present, and the absolutely perfect future.

● **Katz's Other Observations** (A Sampling). (1) Brevity and superficiality are often concomitants. (2) Statements by respected authorities which tend to agree with a writer's viewpoint are always handy. (3) When you are about to do an objective and scientific piece of investigation of a topic, it is well to have the answer firmly in hand, so that you can proceed forthrightly, without being deflected or swayed, directly to the goal.

(All of these were written by Amrom Katz, senior RAND Corp. staff member and until recently assistant director of the Arms Control and Disarmament Agency. The Maxims first appeared in the November, 1967, *Air Force/Space Digest* as part of a much longer article entitled "A Guide for the Perplexed, or a Minimal/Maxim-al Handbook for Tourists in a Classified Bureaucracy." Katz compiled the first five in the 1950s and added six through eight in the 1960s. The "Other Observations" came from three Katz articles: respectively, "Good Disarmament and Bad," *Air Force/Space Digest,* May, 1963; "On Style in R&D," *Air Force/Space Digest,* February, 1962; "A Tribute to George W. Goddard," *Airpower Historian,* October, 1963. *RS.*)

● **Kauffmann's Law.** Authors (and perhaps columnists) eventually rise to the top of whatever depths they were once able to plumb.

(Critic Stanley Kauffman. *JMcC* to *AO.*)

● **Kelley's Law.** Last guys don't finish nice.
(Princeton professor Stanley Kelley, occasioned by the increasing bitterness of political campaigns. *AO.*)

● **Kelly's Law.** An executive will always return to work from lunch early if no one takes him.
(*U.* "Laws to Live By," *The Farmers' Almanac.*)

● **Kennedy's Law.** Excessive official restraints on information are inevitably self-defeating and productive of headaches for the officials concerned.

(Edward Kennedy, AP correspondent best known for his work during World War II. *JW.*)

● **Kent's Law.** The only way a reporter should look at a politician is down.
(From Vic Gold's *P.R. as in President,* Doubleday, 1977, attributed to the *Baltimore Sun*'s Frank Kent.)

● **Kerr-Martin Law.** In dealing with their own problems, faculty members are the most extreme conservatives. In dealing with other people's problems, they are the world's most extreme liberals.
(Clark Kerr.)

● **Kerr's General Rules of Life, Plus Culpability Clause.** (1) Always run a yellow light. (2) Never say no. (3) The younger, the better. *Culpability Clause:* Never admit anything. Never regret anything. Whatever it is, you're not responsible.
(Kerr is a man who works with Sharon Mathews, of Ar-

lington, Va., who collected laws for this collection. She also got the next item from him.)

● **Kerr's Three Rules for Trying New Foods.** (1) Never try anything with tomatoes in it. (2) Never try anything bigger than your head. (3) Never, *never* try anything that looks like vomit . . . then as he says, he broke all three rules by discovering pizza.

● **Kettering's Laws.** (1) If you want to kill any idea in the world today, get a committee working on it. (2) If you have always done it that way, it is probably wrong.
   (Charles F. Kettering, probably the nation's most quotable inventor. *Co.*)

● **Key to Status.** $S = D/K$. S is the status of a person in an organization, D is the number of doors he must open to perform his job and K is the number of keys he carries. A higher number denotes a higher status. Examples: The janitor needs to open 20 doors and has 20 keys ($S = 1$), a secretary has to open two doors with one key ($S = 2$), but the president never has to carry any keys since there is always someone around to open doors for him (with $K = 0$ and a high D, his S reaches infinity).
   (Psychologist Robert Sommer, from his paper "Keys, Kings and Kompanies." See also his *No. 3 Pencil Principle.*)

● **Kharasch's Institutional Imperative.** Every action or decision of an institution must be intended to keep the institution machinery working.
   (Washington lawyer Robert N. Kharasch, from his book *The Institutional Imperative,* Charterhouse Books, 1973. From the basic principle others follow, such as the *Law of Institutional Expertise,* which says, "The expert judg-

ment of an institution, when the matters involve continuation of the institution's operations, is totally predictable, and hence the finding is totally worthless." See also *Security Office, Special Law of. AO.*)

● **Kirkland's Law.** The usefulness of any meeting is in inverse proportion to the attendance.
(AFL-CIO Secretary-Treasurer Lane Kirkland. *AO.*)

● **Kirkup's Law.** The sun goes down just when you need it the most.
(Jon Kirkup. *RS.*)

● **Kitman's Law.** Pure drivel tends to drive ordinary drivel off the TV screen.
(Marvin Kitman, from his book *You Can't Judge a Book by Its Cover,* Weybright and Talley. This law was created at the beginning of the 1967 season in which *The Flying Nun* began its two-year run. In explaining the law, Kitman wrote, "It is inconceivable that three competing networks, working independently in complete secrecy, could produce by accident twenty-six new series so similar in quality.")

● **Knoll's Law of Media Accuracy.** Everything you read in the newspapers is absolutely true except for that rare story of which you happen to have firsthand knowledge.
(Erwin Knoll, editor, *The Progressive.*)

● **Knowles's Law of Legislative Deliberation.** The length of debate varies inversely with the complexity of the issue. *Corollary:* When the issue is simple, and everyone understands it, debate is almost interminable.
(Robert Knowles. *AO.*)

● **Kohn's Second Law.** An experiment is reproducible until another laboratory tries to repeat it.

   (Dr. Alexander Kohn, editor in chief, *JIR,* and Department of Biophysics, Israel Institute for Biological Research. *JIR,* December, 1968.)

● **Koppett's Law.** Whatever creates the greatest inconvenience for the largest number must happen.

   (*U.* From a 1977 Red Smith column, "World Series Rhetoric." Smith says it was first promulgated when "baseball teams began flying around like rice at a wedding in pursuit of the championship of North America.")

● **Kriedt's Law.** Sanity and insanity overlap a fine gray line.

   (Charles van Kriedt, who, according to Laurence J. Peter, reported on a conversation about a politician in which one participant said, "I don't think they could put him in a mental hospital. On the other hand, if he were already in, I don't believe they'd let him out." From the article "Peter's People" in the August, 1976, *Human Behavior.*)

● **Kristol's Law.** Being frustrated is disagreeable, but the real disasters in life begin when you get what you want.

   (Irving Kristol, quoted in George F. Will's *Newsweek* column for November 28, 1977, "Pharaoh in the Promised Land." *JW.*)

● **K Rule.** Words with a *k* in them are funny. If it doesn't have a *k,* it's not funny.

   (Willie Clark, explaining to his nephew why certain things are funny, in Neil Simon's *The Sunshine Boys.* Clark goes on to explain that "chicken" and "pickle" are funny, but "tomato" and "roast beef" are not. This rule is discussed in some detail in Thomas H. Middleton's "Light Refractions'' column in *Saturday Review,* November 13, 1976. Middleton, incidentally, finds some exceptions to the *K Rule,* for example, that ''pike'' is not a terribly funny word but that ''herring'' is.)

L

- **Labor Law.** A disagreeable task is its own reward. (Found posted at the Department of Labor. *TO'B.*)

- **Langin's Law.** If things were left to chance, they'd be better.
  (*U.* Unsigned letter to *Playboy*.)

- **Lani's Principles of Economics.** (1) Taxes are not levied for the benefit of the taxed. (2) $100 placed at 7 percent interest compounded quarterly for 200 years will increase to more than $100,000,000, by which time it will be worth nothing. (3) In God we trust, all others pay cash.
  (*U/S.T.L.*)

- **La Rochefoucauld's Law.** It is more shameful to distrust one's friends than to be deceived by them.
  (Duc de La Rochefoucauld. *S.T.L.*)

- **Late-Comers, Law of.** Those who have the shortest distance to travel to a meeting invariably arrive the latest.
  (Carl Thompson, executive vice-president, Hill and Knowlton. *AO.*)

- **Lawyer's Law.** The phone will not ring until you leave your desk and walk to the other end of the building.
  (Linda A. Lawyer, Pittsburgh.)

- **Lawyer's Rule.** When the law is against you, argue the

facts. When the facts are against you, argue the law. When both are against you, call the other lawyer names.
(*U/ JW.*)

● **Leahy's Law.** If a thing is done wrong often enough, it becomes right. *Corollary:* Volume is a defense to error.
(Richard A. Leahy, Boston. *AO.*)

● **Le Chatellier's Law.** If some stress is brought to bear on a system in equilibrium, the equilibrium is displaced in the direction which tends to undo the effect of the stress.
(Traditional law in the physical sciences that tends to get wide application or, as *Esquire* put it when it listed "Scientific Principles for English Majors," "This may not be one of the all-time essential scientific principles, but it has a certain ring to it.")

● **Ledge's Law of Fans.** (Or, why you can't run when there's trouble in the office.) No matter where you stand, no matter how far or fast you flee, when it hits the fan, as much as possible will be propelled in your direction, and almost none will be returned to the source.
(*U.* John L. Shelton, Dallas.)

● **Lenin's Law.** Whenever the cause of the people is entrusted to professors it is lost.
(Nikolai Lenin. *RS.*)

● **Le Pelley's Law.** The bigger the man, the less likely he is to object to caricature.
(Guernsey Le Pelley, editorial cartoonist for the *Christian Science Monitor,* quoted in the Lewiston, Maine, *Daily Sun,* July 18, 1977.)

● **Levian's Lament.** The fault lies not with our technologies but with our systems.

(Roger Levian, the RAND Corp. *RS.*)

● **Levy's Ten Laws of the Disillusionment of the True Liberal.** (1) Large numbers of things are determined, and therefore not subject to change. (2) Anticipated events never live up to expectations. (3) That segment of the community with which one has the greatest sympathy as a liberal inevitably turns out to be one of the most narrow-minded and bigoted segments of the community.* (4) Always pray that your opposition be wicked. In wickedness there is a strong strain toward rationality. Therefore there is always the possibility, in theory, of handling the wicked by outthinking them. *Corollary 1:* Good intentions randomize behavior. *Subcorollary 1:* Good intentions are far more difficult to cope with than malicious behavior. *Corollary 2:* If good intentions are combined with stupidity, it is impossible to outthink them. *Corollary 3:* Any discovery is more likely to be exploited by the wicked than applied by the virtuous. (5) In unanimity there is cowardice and uncritical thinking. (6) To have a sense of humor is to be a tragic figure. (7) To know thyself is the ultimate form of aggression. (8) No amount of genius can overcome a preoccupation with detail. (9) Only God can make a random selection. (10) Eternal boredom is the price of constant vigilance.

(Marion J. Levy, Jr., chairman of the East Asian studies department, Princeton University. These oft-quoted laws were only nine until recently, and Dr. Levy says, "I have been toying with an 11th. The 11th, if I decide to add it to the 10th, will read as follows, 'Default is more revolutionary than ideals.'")

---

*At this point Levy refers to *Kelley's Law* ("Last guys don't finish nice") as a "reformation" of number 3.

● **Lewis's Law.** People will buy anything that's one to a customer.

> (Sinclair Lewis, quoted by Leo Rosten in his "Diversions" column in *Saturday Review,* May 15, 1976.)

● **Liebling's Law.** If you just try long enough and hard enough, you can always manage to boot yourself in the posterior.

> (A. J. Liebling, in *The Press,* Ballantine Books, 1975.)

● **Lincoln, Ten Points He Did Not Make.** (1) You cannot bring about prosperity by discouraging thrift. (2) You cannot strengthen the weak by weakening the strong. (3) You cannot help small men up by tearing big men down. (4) You cannot help the poor by destroying the rich. (5) You cannot lift the wage-earner up by pulling the wage-payer down. (6). You cannot keep out of trouble by spending more than your income. (7) You cannot further the brotherhood of man by inciting class hatred. (8) You cannot establish sound social security on borrowed money. (9) You cannot build character and courage by taking away a man's initiative and independence. (10) You cannot help men permanently by doing for them what they could and should do for themselves.

> (*Not* Abraham Lincoln. This list of admonitions has been published far and wide—almost always attributed to Lincoln. It has shown up in newspapers, Christmas cards, official documents, the *Congressional Record,* and magazines, with one of the more recent appearances being in the October, 1975, issue of the *Saturday Evening Post.* A May 19, 1950, report from the Library of Congress definitely determined that the ten points were not Lincoln's, but concluded, ". . . there seems to be no way of overtaking the rapid pace with which the mistaken identity has been spreading." To be sure.)

● **Lindy's Law.** The life expectancy of a television comedian is proportional to the total amount of his exposure on the medium.

   (Reported on by Albert Goodman in an article, "Lindy's Law," in *The New Republic,* June 13, 1964. Lindy's, of course, refers to the restaurant where comedians traditionally hang out in New York.)

● **Lloyd-Jones's Law of Leftovers.** The amount of litter on the street is proportional to the local rate of unemployment.
   (David Lloyd-Jones, Tokyo. *AO.*)

● **Local Anesthesia, Law of.** Never say "oops" in the operating room.
   (Dr. Leo Troy.)

● **Loevinger's Law.** Bad news drives good news out of the media.
   (Lee Loevinger, partner, Hogen and Hartson, and former Federal Communications Commission member. An analogue of *Gresham's Law. AO.*)

● **Logg's Rebuttal to Gray's Law of Programming.** $n+1$ trivial tasks take twice as long as n trivial tasks for n sufficiently large.
   (Ed Logg of *S.T.L.*)

● **Longfellow's Elevator Rules.** (1) Face forward. (2) Fold hands in front. (3) Do not make eye contact. (4) Watch the numbers. (5) Don't talk to anyone you don't know. (6) Stop talking with anyone you do know when anyone you don't know enters the elevator. (7). Avoid brushing bodies.
   (Psychologist Layne Longfellow, quoted in *New York,* November 21, 1977, in the article "What New Yorkers

Do in Elevators." Longfellow says we observe these rules "to protect against the possibility of intimate contact.")

● **Long-Range Planning, The (F)law of.** The longer ahead you plan a special event, and the more special it is, the more likely it is to go wrong.

(David and Jayne Evelyn, Arlington, Va.)

● **Long's Notes** (A Handful). (1) Always store beer in a dark place . . . (6) Small change can often be found under seat cushions. (7) It's amazing how much "mature wisdom" resembles being too tired. (8) Secrecy is the beginning of tyranny. (11) An elephant: a mouse built to government specifications. (14) Waking a person unnecessarily should not be considered a capital crime. For a first offense, that is. (17) Rub her feet . . . (21) Never try to outstubborn a cat. (22) Natural laws have no pity. (23) You can go wrong by being too skeptical as readily as by being too trusting . . . (28) A skunk is better company than a person who prides himself on being "frank" . . .

(The main character of *Time Enough for Love: the Further Adventures of Lazurus Long* by Robert A. Heinlein, Putnam, 1973. Long was the oldest human being in the galaxy and his "Notes" were his collected observations and opinions. The "Notes" section of the book has become widely read, quoted, and imitated, especially among science fiction readers. Also see *Short's Quotations.*)

● **Lowrey's Law.** If it jams . . . force it. If it breaks, it needed replacing anyway.

(*U/Scientific Collections.*)

● **Lowrey's Law of Expertise.** Just when you get really good at something, you don't need to do it anymore.

(William P. Lowrey, Sidney, Ill. *HW.*)

● **Lubin's Law.** If another scientist thought your research was more important than his, he would drop what he is doing and do what you are doing.

> (From the law collection of William K. Wright, administrative officer, Naval Health Research Center, San Diego, Cal.)

● **Luce's Law.** No good deed goes unpunished.
> (Clare Boothe Luce.)

● **Luten's Laws.** (1) When properly administered, vacations do not diminish productivity: for every week you're away and get nothing done, there's another when your boss is away and you get twice as much done. (2) It's not so hard to lift yourself by your bootstraps once you're off the ground!
> (Daniel B. Luten, Berkeley, Cal. *AO.*)

● **Lynott's Law of the Reverse Learning Curve.** Wisdom and knowledge decrease in inverse proportion to age.
> (William J. Lynott, Abington, Pa. *AO.* The proof of this law, according to its author, comes when you engage in conversation with someone younger than yourself and find that person knows far more about any subject than you do.)

- **Maier's Law.** If facts do not conform to the theory, they must be disposed of.

    (N. R. F. Maier first announced this oft-quoted law in the March, 1960, issue of *American Psychologist*. At that time he also revealed that psychologists commonly obey the law by [a] failing to report the facts, or [b] giving them a new name.)

- **Malek's Law.** Any simple idea will be worded in the most complicated way.

    (*Sig Malek/S.T.L.*)

- **Mankiewicz's Laws.** *Law of Crowds:* The more enthusiastic, unruly, and large the candidate's crowds in the week before the election, the less likely he is to carry the area, cf. JFK in Ohio. *Environmental Law:* People who are excessively concerned about the environment invariably turn out to own a great deal of land. There are damn few unemployed and renters in the ecology movement. *Law of Provincial Hotels:* The amount of quaint, authentic, rustic charm varies inversely with the pounds per square inch of water pressure in the shower. High charm, low pressure. *School Law:* The higher the tuition, the fewer days they spend in school. *Second Law of Politics:* A politician will always tip off his true belief by stating the opposite at the beginning of the sentence. For maximum comprehension, do not start listening until the first clause is concluded. Begin instead at the word "but" which begins the second—or active—clause. This is the way to tell a liberal from a conservative—before they tell you. Thus: "I have always believed in a strong national defense, second to none, but . . . (a liberal, about to propose a $20 billion cut in the defense budget).

> (Frank Mankiewicz, president of National Public Radio and formerly press secretary to the 1972 McGovern campaign. The *Second Law of Politics* originally appeared in the *Washingtonian,* July, 1975. As for his *First Law of Politics,* he explains, "All of my laws of politics are 'second' on the theory that I will find a better one.")

● **Man's Law.** No matter what happens, there is always somebody who knew that it would.

> (*U/"LSP."*)

● **Marcus's Law.** The number of letters written to the editor is inversely proportional to the importance of the article.

> (Robert L. Marcus, Scarsdale, N.Y., in a letter published in *The New York Times* on April 7, 1968. It was in response to the "Faber's Law" article, which had occasioned a number of letters. *FD.*)

● **Marshall's Generalized Iceberg Theorem.** Seven-eighths of everything can't be seen.

> (*U/S.T.L.*)

● **Marshall's Universal Laws of Perpetual Perceptual Obfuscation.** (1) Nobody perceives anything with total accuracy. (2) No two people perceive the same thing identically. (3) Few perceive what difference it makes . . . or care.

> (Jack A. Marshall, Arlington, Mass. *AO.*)

● **Martin's Basic Laws of Instant Analysis.** (1) *The Law of Nondefinition*: If it is generally known what one is supposed to be doing, then someone will expect him to do it. (2) *The Law of Minimum Effort:* In any given group, the most will do the least and the least the most. (3) *The Law of Augmented Complexity:*

There is nothing so simple that it cannot be made difficult. (4) *The Law of Nonresponsibility:* In any given miscalculation, the fault will never be placed if more than one person is involved. (5) *The Law of Prior Menace:* People see what they have been conditioned to see; they refuse to see what they don't expect to see. (6) *The Law of Randomness:* Consistency is the product of small minds. (Paraphrasing Emerson on the "hobgoblin of little minds.") (7) *The Law of Instant Response:* A quick response is worth a thousand logical responses.

> (Merle P. Martin, Anchorage, Alaska, in his 1975 *Journal of Systems Management* article entitled "The Instant Analyst." Martin, a systems analyst, uses the article to reveal the secrets of that profession—or, at least, the instant version. One of the highlights of the piece is the collection of "instant phrases" Martin suggests to use when applying the *Law of Instant Response.* Among others, he sanctions the use of: "Don't stop to stomp ants when the elephants are stampeding," "That's only true because it's true," "That is utterly preposterous," and "Trust me!" RS.)

● **Martin's Definition of Drunkenness.** You're not drunk if you can lie on the floor without holding on.
(Dean Martin. *S.T.L.*)

● **Martin's Laws, Principles, Effects, Plagiarisms, etc.** *The Martin-Berthelot Principle*: Of all possible committee reactions to any given agenda item, the reaction that will occur is the one which will liberate the greatest amount of hot air. *Martin's Laws of Academia:* (1) The faculty expands its activity to fit whatever space is available, so that more space is always required. (2) Faculty purchases of equipment and supplies always increase to match the funds available, so these funds are never adequate. (3) The professional quality of the faculty tends to be inversely proportional to the importance it attaches to space and equipment. *Martin's Law of Committees:* All committee reports conclude that "it is not prudent to change the policy [or procedure, or organization, or whatever] at this time." *Martin's Exclusion:* Committee reports dealing with wages, salaries, fringe benefits, facilities, computers, employee parking, libraries, coffee breaks, secretarial support, etc., always call for dramatic expenditure increases. *Martin's Law of Communication:* The inevitable result of improved and enlarged communication between different levels in a hierarchy is a vastly increased area of misunderstanding. *Martin's Laws of Hierarchical Function:* (1) All hierarchies contain administrators and managers, and they tend to appear at alternating levels in the hierarchy. (2) Administration maintains the status quo. (3) Management directs and controls change. *Martin's Minimax Maxim:* Everyone knows that the name of the game is to let the other guy have all of the little tats and to keep all of the big tits for yourself. *Martin's Plagiarism of H. L. Mencken:* Those who can—do. Those who cannot—teach. Those who cannot teach become deans.

(Thomas L. Martin, Jr., from *Malice in Blunderland,* McGraw-Hill, 1971.)

● **Matsch's Maxim.** A fool in high station is like a man on the top of a high mountain: everything appears small to him and he appears small to everybody.
(Professor Leader W. Matsch.)

● **May's Mordant Maxim.** A university is a place where men of principle outnumber men of honor.
(Historian Ernest May. *AO.*)

● **McCarthy's Law of Intelligence.** Being in politics is like being a football coach. You have to be smart enough to understand the game and dumb enough to think it's important.
(Eugene McCarthy. *MBC's Laws of Politics.*)

● **McClaughry's Iron Law of Zoning.** When it's not needed, zoning works fine; when it is essential, it always breaks down.

> (John McClaughry, Concord, Vt. The law was born when McClaughry was studying the effects of zoning in the course of the 1974 debate on the Vermont Land Use Plan. As he explains, "A speaker had urged state zoning to 'keep Vermont from turning into Los Angeles.' When it was pointed out that Los Angeles had had zoning in force since 1923, McClaughry's Iron Law rapidly emerged. I was at the time chairman of the Planning Commission of Kirby, Vermont, population 230, which had zoning but absolutely no need for it since there was no development pressure.")

● **McClaughry's Law of Public Policy.** Politicians who vote huge expenditures to alleviate problems get reelected; those who propose structural changes to prevent problems get early retirement.

> (John McClaughry.)

● **McClaughry's Second Law.** Liberals, but not conservatives, can get attention and acclaim for denouncing liberal policies that failed; and liberals will inevitably capture the ensuing agenda for "reform."

> (McClaughry again.)

● **McGovern's Law.** The longer the title, the less important the job.

> (Robert Shrum, who was one of George McGovern's speechwriters, recalled this law for *AO*. McGovern discovered the law in 1960, when President Kennedy tried to persuade him that being director of the Food for Peace Program was a more influential job than secretary of agriculture.)

● **McGurk's Law.** Any improbable event which would create maximum confusion if it did occur, will occur.

   (H. S. Kindler, from *Organizing the Technical Conference,* Reinhold Publishing Co., 1960. McGurk, no doubt, is Murphy's first cousin.)

● **McKenna's Law.** When you are right be logical, when you are wrong be-fuddle.

   (Gerard E. McKenna, president, Gerard E. McKenna & Associates, Middle Grove, N.Y.)

● **McLandress's Theorems of Business Confidence.** (1) The confidence of the business executive in a President is inversely related to the state of business. (2) Government action and inaction both gravely impair business confidence. (3) Reassurance of business by a President has an unfavorable effect on confidence. (4) Unkind words do not enhance business confidence. (5) That politics has a bearing on business confidence is unproven.

   (Mark Epernay, in *The McLandress Dimension,* Houghton Mifflin, 1962. By way of explanation, if one thinks of Herbert Hoover the theorems come into better focus. For example, no modern president enjoyed the level of business confidence that Hoover did [Theorem (1)], and the only time that he did not enjoy that confidence was in 1930 and 1931, after he tried to reassure them [Theorem (3)].

   Epernay's book reveals and discusses many other theories first offered by the legendary but mythical Dr. Herschel McLandress. For instance the "Dimension" mentioned in the title is a measure of human behavior determined by finding "the arithmetic mean or average of the intervals of time during which a subject's thoughts remained centered on some substantive phenomenon other than his own personality." Art Buchwald, for instance, has a high score of two hours, Norman Cousins, three minutes, and Richard Nixon, one of the lowest, at three seconds.

In case you have not heard of Epernay, the author of this book, some light was shed on the matter when a Christmas card was found tucked in a used edition of the book:

Dec 16.
Dear ———,

We hope that you both enjoy this "spoof," we have. There is a strong rumor around Cambridge that "Mark Epernay" is a pen name for John Kenneth Galbraith. That seems plausible. This is not what I hoped to be able to send.)

● **McLaughlin's Law.** The length of any meeting is inversely proportional to the length of the agenda for that meeting. (G. Robert McLaughlin, John Hancock Mutual Life Insurance Co., Boston. *AO.*)

● **McNaughton's Rule.** Any argument worth making within the bureaucracy must be capable of being expressed in a single declarative sentence that is obviously true once stated.
(The late John McNaughton, a government national security expert. It was sent to *AO* by Harvard political scientist Graham Allison.)

● **Meditz Subway Phenomenon.** No matter which train you are waiting for, the wrong one comes first.
(J. R. Meditz, New York City.)

● **Melcher's Law.** In a bureaucracy every routing slip will expand until it contains the maximum number of names that can be typed in a single vertical column, namely, twenty-seven.
(Daniel Melcher. *JW.*)

● **Mencken's Law.** Whenever A annoys or injures B on the pretense of saving or improving X, A is a scoundrel.

(H. L. Mencken. Joe Goulden, writer and student of Mencken, reports that this appeared in Mencken's *Newspaper Days* as "Mencken's Law," but that it was derived from "the Law of the Forgotten Man," found in "The Absurd Effort to Make the World Over," *The Forum*, XVII, 1894, by the Social Darwinist William Graham Sumner, to wit, "When A and B join to make a law to help X, their law always proposes to decide what C shall do for X, and C is the Forgotten Man." Mencken acknowledged his debt to Sumner, but still called his version "Mencken's Law." Goulden adds that Mencken had another version that concludes, ". . . A is a scoundrel, and should be briskly clubbed." Still another variation appeared in a recent column by James J. Kilpatrick where it was termed "Mencken's Working Hypothesis of the Legislative Process" and stated as: "Whenever A attempts by law to impose his moral standards on B, A is most likely a scoundrel.")

● **Mencken's Meta-law.** For every human problem, there is a neat, plain solution—and it is always wrong.

(H. L. Mencken. *AO.*)

● **Merrill's First Corollary.** There are no winners in life; only survivors.

(*U/S.T.L.*)

● **Meskimen's Laws of Bureaucracies.** (1) When they want it bad (in a rush), they get it bad. (2) There's never time to do it right but always time to do it over.

(John K. Meskimen, Falls Church, Va. *AO.*)

● **Mesmerisms of Review and Control, The Twelve.** (1) First, in order to keep engineers and scientists cognizant of the importance of progress, load them down with forms, multiple reports, and frequent meetings. (2) Remember, the more engineering projects there are, the more products there will be. (3) . . . the less management demands of engineers and scientists, the greater their productivity. (4) Computer-based management information systems will cure most review and control problems. (5) The greater the number of professionals (advanced degrees preferred) assigned to a project, the greater the progress. (6) . . . cost consciousness and sophisticated design are basically incompatible. (7) If enough reports are prepared and technical reviews are held, negative information will always filter its way to senior management. (8) . . . high salaries equals happiness equals project progress. (9) The expenditure of funds is critical—engineers and scientists should not be permitted to authorize any purchase. (10) Scientists and engineers set high performance standards for themselves; therefore, performance appraisal and career planning are perfunctory. (11) Since blue-sky projects are targeted for major breakthroughs, they are relatively immune from effective planning and control. (12) Vastly improved review and control will result by promoting the most productive engineers and scientists to management positions.

(Richard F. Moore, the National Cash Register Co., Dayton, Ohio. *JIR,* January, 1973.)

● **Metz's Rules of Golf for Good Players** (Whose Scores Would Reflect Their True Ability If Only They Got an Even Break Once in Awhile) (1) On beginning play, as many balls as may be required to obtain a satisfactory result may be played from the first tee. Everyone recognizes a good player needs to "loosen up" but does not not have time for the practice tee. (2) A ball sliced or hooked into the rough shall be lifted and placed in the fairway at a point equal to the distance it carried or rolled in the rough. Such veering right or left frequently results from friction between the face of the club and the cover of the ball, and the player should not be penalized for erratic behavior of the ball resulting from such uncontrollable mechanical phenomena. (3) A ball hitting a tree shall be deemed not to have hit the tree. Hitting a tree is simply bad luck and has no place in a scientific game. The player should estimate the distance the ball would have traveled if it had not hit the tree and play the ball from there, preferably from atop a nice firm tuft of grass. (4) There shall be no such thing as a lost ball. The missing ball is on or near the course somewhere and eventually will be found and pocketed by someone else. It thus becomes a stolen ball, and the player should not compound the felony by charging himself with a penalty stroke. (5) When played from a sand trap, a ball which does not clear the trap on being struck maybe hit again on the roll without counting an extra stroke. In no case will more than two strokes be counted in playing from a trap, since it is only reasonable to assume that if the player had time to concentrate on his shot, instead of hurrying it so as not to delay his playing partners, he would be out in two. (6) If a putt passes over the hole without dropping, it is deemed to have dropped. The law of gravity holds that any object attempting to maintain a position in the atmosphere without something to support it must drop. The law of gravity supercedes the law of golf. (7) Same thing goes for a ball that stops at the brink of the hole and hangs there, defying gravity. You cannot defy the law. (8) Same thing goes for a ball that rims the cup. A ball should not go sideways. This violates the laws of physics. (9) A putt that stops close enough to the cup to inspiresuchcommentsas"you could   blow   it   in"   may   be   blown   in. This rule does not apply if the ball is more than three inches from the hole, because no one wants to make a travesty of the game.

(Donald A. Metz, Devon, Pa.)

● **Michehl's Theorem.** Less is more.
(*U/S.T.L.* See *Pastore's Comment on Michehl's Theorem.*)

● **Miles's Law.** Where you stand depends on where you sit.

>(Rufus Miles, former career administrator at the Department of Health, Education and Welfare, to express the fact that your opinion depends on your job. Appeared in *AO*'s column and elsewhere. Has become one of Robert Machol's *POR.*)

● **Miller's Law. [J.]** Unless you put your money to work for you—you work for your money.

>(Joe Miller. Fort Myers, Fla.)

● **Miller's Law.[M.]** The yoo-hoo you yoo-hoo into the forest is the yoo-hoo you get back.

>(Merle Miller. *RS.*)

● **Miller's Law.[N.]** The corruption in a country is in inverse proportion to its state of development.

>(Nathan Miller, Chevy Chase, Md. *AO.*)

● **Miller's Law.[?]** You can't tell how deep a puddle is until you step into it.

>(*U/S.T.L.*)

● **Mills's Law of Transportation Logistics.** The distance to the gate from which your flight departs is inversely proportionate to the time remaining before the scheduled departure of the flight.

>(Edward S. Mills, National Association of Blue Shield Plans, *AO.*)

● **Money, The Natural Law of.** Anything left over today will be needed tomorrow to pay an unexpected bill.

>(Betty Canary, in her *Surviving as a Woman,* Henry Regnery Publishing, 1976.)

● **Montagu's Maxim.** The idea is to die young as late as possible.
> (Anthropologist Ashley Montagu. *MLS.*)

● **Morley's Conclusion.** No man is lonely while eating spaghetti.
> (Robert Morley.)

● **Mosher's Law.** It's better to retire too soon than too late.
> (Representative Charles A. Mosher [R-Ohio], on retiring at seventy after sixteen years in Congress. *JW.*)

● **Mother Sigafoos's Observation.** A man should be greater than some of his parts.
> (Uttered by a character of the same name in Peter De Vries's *I Hear America Swinging. RS.*)

● **Moynihan's Law.** If the newspapers of a country are filled with good news, the jails will be filled with good people.
> (Senator Daniel P. Moynihan. *JW.*)

● **Mudgeeraba Creek Emu-Riding and Boomerang-Throwing Association, Rule of the.** Decisions of the judges will be final unless shouted down by a really overwhelming majority of the crowd present. Abusive and obscene language may not be used by contestants when addressing members of the judging panel, or, conversely, by members of the judging panel when addressing contestants (unless struck by a boomerang).
> (From Benjamin Ruhe's *Many Happy Returns: The Art and Sport of Boomeranging,* Viking, 1977. The rule was created to underscore the informality and casualness of boomerang competition.)

● **Munnecke's Law.** If you don't say it, they can't repeat it.

(Wilbur C. Munnecke, quoted in a letter to Ann Landers from one "Benton Harbor Ben.")

● **Murchison's Law of Money.** Money is like manure. If you spread it around, it does a lot of good. But if you pile it up in one place, it stinks like hell.
(Clint Murchison, Jr., Texas financier, repeating his father's advice. *Time,* June 16, 1971.)

Murphy's Law(s).
The importance of *Murphy's Law(s)* in contemporary American society is such that:
○   In late 1977, when things were not going particularly well at the White House, a set of *Murphy's Laws* was sent to all of the President's aides. According to the *Washingtonian,* which reported it, all the notes were signed J.C.
○   Serious business and scientific periodicals discuss important issues in terms of Murphy ("A Partial Repeal of Murphy's Law" was a recent *Business Week* article title), and he has become the darling of newspaper columnists, who apply his findings to help explain an altogether imperfect world.
Because of the once and future importance of *Murphy's Law(s),* the subject is worthy of more than passing attention. Therefore, let us examine the Murphy phenomenon by addressing some basic questions.

EXACTLY WHAT ARE MURPHY'S LAWS AND IN WHAT ORDER SHOULD
THEY BE LISTED?

Having examined dozens of printed, typewritten, and
Xeroxed listings of *Murphy's Laws,* we can report that no two are
exactly alike. Even those which at first appear to have been
copied by hand from one another tend to show discrepancies in
order, phrasing, or both. (This is, of course, a direct confirmation
of Murphian theory.) If there is any semblance of consistency, it
is with the first and ninth laws, which are the same on a number
of lists but not all. This confusion is so pervasive and in the spirit
of Murphy that it seems to have mystic overtones—one expects
that if you Xeroxed enough copies of a given list, eventually one
would emerge with a glitch in it.

Lacking an "official" listing, here is the author's collection

Murphy's Laws.

1. If anything can go wrong, it will.
2. Nothing is ever as simple as it seems.
3. Everything takes longer than you expect.
4. If there is a possibility of several things going wrong,
the one that will go wrong first will be the one that will do the
most damage.
5. Left to themselves, all things go from bad to worse.
6. If you play with something long enough, you will
surely break it.
7. If everything seems to be going well, you have obviously overlooked something.
8. If you see that there are four possible ways in which
a procedure can go wrong, and circumvent these, then a fifth
way, unprepared for, will promptly develop.
9. Nature always sides with the hidden flaw.
10. Mother Nature is a bitch.
11. It is impossible to make anything foolproof, because
fools are so ingenious.
12. If a great deal of time has been expended seeking the

answer to a problem with the only result being failure, the answer will be immediately obvious to the first unqualified person.

IS THAT ALL? IT SEEMS AS IF I RECALL OTHERS.

Using the basic laws for inspiration, all sorts of corollaries, amendments, and specialized laws follow. A sampling:

> *Murphy's Law of Thermodynamics.* Things get worse under pressure. (*S.T.L.*)

Royster's Refinement of Murphy's Law. When things go wrong somewhere, they are apt to go wrong everywhere. (Vermont Royster, in *The Wall Street Journal.*)

Murphy's Law of Priorities. Whatever you want to do, you have to do something else first. (Art Kosatka, a staff assistant to Rep. John M. Murphy [!] of New York, quoted in Bill Gold's column in *The Washington Post,* March 7, 1978.)

Murphy's Law of the Open Road. When there is a very long road upon which there is a one-way bridge placed at random and there are two cars only on that road, it follows that: (1) the two cars are going in opposite directions and (2) they will always meet at the bridge. (B. D. Firstbrook, Westmount, Quebec. *AO.*)

Barton's Amendment to Murphy's Law. . . . and even if it can't, it might. (A. J. Barton, The National Science Foundation.)

Murphy's Laws of College Publishing. (1) Availability of manuscripts in a given subject area is inversely proportional to the need for books in that area. (2) A manuscript for a market in which no textbooks currently exist will be followed two weeks after contracting by an announcement of an identical book by your closest competitor. (*Computer Science News,* December, 1972.)

Murphy's Law of Copiers. The legibility of a copy is inversely proportional to its importance. (Letter to *AO* from G. H. Brandenburger, Butte, Mont., containing illegible photocopy of *Murphy's Laws.*)

Crowell's Law. Murphy's Law never fail∾ (Walter J. Crowell, Bethpage, N.Y.)

Warren's Law. The likelihood of anything happening is in direct proportion to the amount of trouble it will cause if it does happen. (Sam W. Warren, editor and publisher, *The Northside Sun,* Jackson, Miss.)

The Yulish Additions. ■Persons disagreeing with your facts are always emotional and employ faulty reasoning. ■ Enough research will tend to confirm your conclusions. ■ The more urgent the need for decision, the less apparent becomes the identity of the decision-maker. ■The more complex the idea or technology, the more simpleminded is the opposition. ■Each profession talks to itself in its own unique language. Apparently there is no Rosetta Stone. (From a collection of "Murphy's Fundamental Laws" published by Charles Yulish Associates, Inc., of New York, 1975.)

API Corollary. If things can go wrong, they will—and when they do, blame it on the oil industry. (Law created by an American Petroleum Institute spokesman when the oil industry got blamed for creating snafus associated with delegates checking in for the National Women's Conference in Houston. The API claimed it checked out two days earlier.)

Murphy's Laws of Analysis. (1) In any collection of data, the figures that are obviously correct will contain errors. (2) It is customary for a decimal to be misplaced. (3) An error that can creep into a calculation, will. Also, it will always be in the direction that will cause the most damage to the calculation. (Three of twenty-nine laws that appear in G. C. Beakly's *Introduction to Engineering Design and Graphics,* Macmillan, 1975.)

Murphy's Law and Correlative Collegiate Cabalae. (1) During an exam, the pocket calculator battery will fail. (2) If only one parking space is available it will have a blue curb.* (3) Exams will always contain questions not discussed in class.

(4) All students who obtain a B will feel cheated out of an A. (5) Campus sidewalks never exist as the straightest line between two points. (6) When a pencil point breaks, the nearest sharpener is exactly 1,000 feet away. (7) At five minutes before the hour, a student will ask a question requiring a ten minute answer. (8) If a course requires a prerequisite, a student will not have had it. (9) The office space and salaries of college administrators are in inverse proportion to those of the instructors. (10) Slightly deaf students will have instructors who mumble. (11) The next class is always three buildings away on a rainy day. (12) He who can will. He who can't, will teach. (13) When a student actually does a homework problem, the instructor will not ask for it. (14) All math classes begin at 8 A.M.; also, movies on Federal Government. (15) Students who obtain an A for a course will claim that the instructor is a great teacher. (16) If an instructor says, "It is obvious," it won't be. (17) When wool sweaters are worn, classroom temperatures are 95 degrees Fahrenheit. (18) If a student has to study, he will claim that the course is unfair. (19) Ambidextrous instructors will erase with one hand while writing with the other. (20) An A is easily obtained if a student calls the instructor "Professor." (21) When slides are shown in a darkened room, the instructor will require students to take notes. (22) When . . . then . . . (You fill in the blanks.) (M. M. "Johnny" Johnston, Ormond Beach, Fla.)

WHO WAS MURPHY ANYHOW?

Good question. The Murphy Center devoted considerable time and expense to this question. Various approaches were taken, including, for instance, contacting a fair sampling of Murphys, such as Patrick V. Murphy, former New York City police commissioner and present director of the Police Foundation in Washington. He, along with the other Murphys contacted, had

---

*Not prohibitions against X-rated movies, but curbs painted blue and reserved for "STAFF."

no idea who the original lawmaker was. Nor, for that matter, were any meaningful clues unearthed through a study of famous Murphys, including possibilities as promising as William Lawrence Murphy (1876–1959), the inventor and man who gave his name to the fabled folding bed.

However, some interesting theories and clues emerged from the quest, including the following:

The Kilroy Theory. Like those kingpins of World War II folklore, Kilroy and Murgatroyd the Kluge Maker, one body of thought concludes that somewhere along the line there *may or may not* have been a real Murphy, but that this is beside the point.* The point is that Murphy has come to represent a spirit and presence that transcends one human being. If one accepts this, then virtually any accounting works, whether it be the Edsel Murphy of the engineering magazines or the Finn Cool O'Murphy who allegedly recorded his rules on a runic scroll in the first century A.D.

The Knoll Shul Theory. To quote, "I'm afraid I can only offer you a conjecture about the original Murphy. Thirty years ago, when I lived in the Crown Heights section of Brooklyn, the neighborhood synagogue was widely known (at least among the young hoodlums with whom I consorted) as Murphy's Shul. I have no idea who that Murphy was, or how he happened to lend his name to an orthodox synagogue, but I have always assumed— since first I encountered Murphy's Law—that it must be the same Murphy. Somehow it figures."†

---

*Kilroy was a household name during the war, and the line "Kilroy was here" appeared everywhere from the hulls of battleships to the tattooed chests of sailors. There were many theories as to who he was, but none stuck. He was represented by this: Murgatroyd was a young man who finagled himself a nice billet on a ship as a "Kluge maker." He got away without doing anything for a long time, but finally, on the occasion of an admiral's visit, he was told to make a Kluge to impress the VIP. He worked all night, and just as the admiral arrived he ran up on deck, started to present it, tripped, and it fell overboard. As it sank it went, "Kluge."
†Erwin Knoll, editor of *The Progressive,* in a letter to the author.

The Great Teacher Theory. To quote, "One day a teacher named Murphy wanted to demonstrate the laws of probability to his math class. He had thirty of his students spread peanut butter on slices of bread, then toss the bread into the air to see if half would fall on the dry side and half on the buttered side. As it turned out, twenty-nine of the slices landed peanut-butter side on the floor, while the thirtieth stuck to the ceiling."*

The Yulish Blur Hypothesis. An exhaustive search by a New York consulting firm concluded that Murphy (a) had no first name, (b) could not hold a job, (c) never prepared a résumé. Little else was known about him.†

While all of these theories are worth considering, the real story may have recently come to light without great fanfare. On January 13, 1977, Jack Smith, a columnist for the *Los Angeles Times,* revealed that he had gotten a letter from George E. Nichols of the Jet Propulsion Laboratory in Pasadena stating that he not only knew the origin of the law but the true identity of Murphy. According to the Nichols letter, "The event [that led to the naming of the law] occurred in 1949 at Edwards Air Force Base . . . during Air Force Project MX981 . . . The law [was named after] Capt. Ed Murphy, a development engineer from Wright Field [Ohio] Aircraft Lab. Frustration with a strap transducer that was malfunctioning due to an error in wiring the strain gauge bridges caused him to remark [of the technician who had wired the bridges at the lab], 'If there is any way to do it wrong, he will.' I assigned the name Murphy's Law to that statement and the associated variations."

Nichols went on to point out that the law was off and running after it was alluded to in a press conference a few weeks later. A similar letter appeared in late 1977 in Arthur Bloch's book *Murphy's Law.* Further detail on Project MX981 and Murphy

*Letter to William and Mary Morris from Gary M. Klauber of Silver Spring, Md. It appears in their *Dictionary of Word and Phrase Origins,* Vol. III, Harper & Row, 1971. The Morrises solicited theories on Murphy through their newspaper column.
†Press release from the firm of Charles Yulish Associates in New York.

were supplied to the author when he contacted Robert J. Smith, Chief of the History Office at Wright-Patterson Air Force Base. Smith was unable to confirm the actual naming but was able to supply information on Murphy—graduated from West Point in 1940, was a pilot as well as an engineer, worked on a number of research projects and would be sixty years old today. The mysterious-sounding MX981 was intended "to study the factors in human tolerance to high decelerative forces of short duration in order to determine criteria for design of aircraft and protective equipment." As Smith adds, "If this project gave birth to Murphy's Law, hopefully, the consequences were minor."

DO YOU BELIEVE THIS?

Yes, as a matter of fact, but there is still much to be said for the Kilroy theory, which says that if Ed Murphy had not discovered *Murphy's Law,* someone else would have. Then again, one of the many corollaries to *Murphy's Law* states that on the rare occasion on which something is successful, the wrong person gets the credit.

ARE THERE OTHER NAMES FOR MURPHY'S LAW?

Certainly. Other names include "Thermodamnics," "Snafu Theory," and "Klugemanship." One should also be aware of the name D. L. Klipstein, who has worked out several score corollaries for engineers. Also see the entries in this book for Finagle, O'Toole, and Sod.

●   **Murstein's Law.** The amount of research devoted to a topic in human behavior is inversely proportional to its importance and interest.

(Bernard I. Murstein. *JW.*)

N

● **Nader's Law.** The speed of exit of a civil servant is directly proportional to the quality of his service.

> (Ralph Nader, from *The Spoiled System,* a study of the Civil Service Commission by a Nader task force. *AO.*)

● **NASA Truisms.** (1) Research is reading two books that have never been read in order to write a third that will never be read. (2) A consultant is an ordinary person a long way from home. (3) Statistics are a highly logical and precise method for saying a half-truth inaccurately.

> (From a file in the NASA archives on "Humor and Satire.")

● **Nations, Law of.** In an underdeveloped country, don't drink the water; in a developed country, don't breathe the air.

> (An item that originally appeared in *Changing Times* and was quoted in the *Reader's Digest* of June, 1976.)

● **Navy Law.** If you can keep your head when all about you others are losing theirs, maybe you just don't understand the situation.

> (Traditional sign that has been showing up on ships and offices of the U.S. Navy for years. It is found elsewhere, too, but is primarily associated with the Navy.)

● **Nessen's Law.** Secret sources are more credible.
(Ron Nessen, President Ford's press secretary, who was quoted in *Newsweek,* January 31, 1977: "Some statements you make in public . . . are reported as . . . an unnamed source . . . Nobody believes the official spokes-

man . . . but everybody trusts an unidentified source." From the latest version of Martin Krakowski's paper "Anthropogenic Ills.")

● **Newton's Little-Known Seventh Law.** A bird in the hand is safer than two overhead.
(*U/S.T.L.*)

● **Nienberg's Law.** Progress is made on alternate Fridays.
(*U/S.T.L.*)

● **Nies's Law.** The effort expended by the bureaucracy in defending any error is in direct proportion to the size of the error.
(John Nies, Washington patent lawyer and *AO*'s neighbor.)

● **Ninety-Nine Rule of Project Schedules.** The first 90 percent of the task takes 90 percent of the time, the last 10 percent takes the other 90 percent.
(*Co.*)

● **Nixon's Principle.** If two wrongs don't make a right, try three.
(Lawrence J. Peter. *MLS.*)

● **Nobel Effect.** There is no proposition, no matter how foolish, for which a dozen Nobel signatures cannot be collected. Furthermore, any such petition is guaranteed page-one treatment in *The New York Times*.
(Daniel S. Greenberg, from his *Science and Government Report,* December, 1976. *RS.*)

● **Noble's Law of Political Imagery.** All other things being equal, a bald man cannot be elected President of the United States. *Corollary:* Given a choice between two bald political candidates, the American people will vote for the less bald of the two.

> (Bald writer Vic Gold in his *Washingtonian* article "Can a Bald Man Be Elected President?" Noble is G. Vance Noble, author of *The Hirsute Tradition in American Politics,* widely believed to be one of Gold's alter egos.)

● **Nofziger's Law of Details.** The American people aren't interested in details.

> (Lyn Nofziger of Ronald Reagan's campaign staff, on such matters as Senator Barry Goldwater giving analyses of such things as the comparative defense capabilities of a General Dynamics prototype aircraft *vs.* Boeing's model. From Vic Gold's *P.R. as in President.* See *Spencer's [Contradictory] Corollary.*)

● **North Carolina Equine Paradox.** VYARZERZOMANIMOR ORSEZASSEZANZERAREORSES?

> (Sign seen on the walls of print shops in North Carolina, reported to *AO* by Carl Thompson of Hill and Knowlton.)

● **No. 3 Pencil Principle.** Make it sufficiently difficult for people to do something, and most people will stop doing it. *Corollary:* If no one uses something, it isn't needed.

> (Another important discovery from psychologist Robert Sommer. He discovered the principle when he worked for a government agency and his office manager decided to ban soft, comfortable-to-use No. 2 pencils and order No. 3s, which are scratchy and write light. Pencil consumption in the office went down and the office manager was able to prove that No. 3s "last longer." Sommer revealed his finding in the December, 1973, issue of *Worm Runner's Digest.*)

● **Nyquist's Theory of Equilibrium.** Equality is not when a female Einstein gets promoted to assistant professor; equality is when a female schlemiel moves ahead as fast as a male schlemiel.

(Ewald Nyquist. *RS.*)

● **Oaks's Unruly Laws for Lawmakers.** (1) Law expands in proportion to the resources available for its enforcement. (2) Bad law is more likely to be supplemented than repealed. (3) Social legislation cannot repeal physical laws.

（Dallin B. Oaks, president of Brigham Young University and president of the American Association of Presidents of Independent Colleges and Universities. The laws appeared in an essay, "Unruly Laws for Lawmakers," by Oaks which appeared in *The Congressional Record* for March 17, 1978. Oaks, who makes no effort to hide his bias against lawmaking as the solution to all problems, also uses the essay to list three hypotheses which have come out of his research on the first law: [1] The public is easily fooled by government claims of economizing. [2] An uninformed lawmaker is more likely to produce a complicated law than a simple one. [3] Bad or complicated law tends to drive out good judgment.）

● **O'Brien's First Law of Politics.** The more campaigning, the better.

（Larry O'Brien, who stated it when he ran John F. Kennedy's campaign in 1960. *FL.*）

● **O'Brien's Law.** If an editor can reject your paper, he will. *Corollary:* If you submit the paper to a second editor, his journal invariably demands an entirely different reference system.

（Maeve O'Connor of *The British·Medical Journal* on discovering at least 2,632 possible ways of setting out references in scientific articles. Named for O'Brien, who is first cousin to Murphy.）

● **O'Brien's Principle (aka The $357.63 Theory).** Auditors always reject any newsman's expense account with a bottom line divisible by 5 or 10.

(Named for Emmet N. O'Brien and passed along to *AO* by Jake Underhill of the New York Life Insurance Co. Underhill worked for O'Brien, as did Germond of *Germond's Law*. *O'Brien's*, *Germond's*, and *Weaver's laws* form a set that came of research conducted around Albany, New York, in the early 1950s. Underhill terms the experience the "Albany Reportorial School of Economics." See also *O'Doyle's Corollary*.)

● **O'Brien's Rule.** Nothing is ever done for the right reasons.

(*U/"LSP."*)

● **Occam's Electric Razor.** The most difficult light bulb to replace burns out first and most frequently.
(Writer Joe Anderson.)

● **Occam's Razor.** Entities ought not to be multiplied except from necessity.

(William of Occam, a fourteenth-century scholar, whose call to keep things simple has many modern incarnations, including the following:
• "The explanation requiring the fewest assumptions is the most likely to be correct." *JW*.
• "Whenever two hypotheses cover the facts, use the simpler of the two." *Forbes*.
• "Cut the crap." *Esquire*.)

● **O'Doyle's Corollary.** No matter how many reporters share a cab, and no matter who pays, each puts the full fare on his own expense account.
(Edward P. O'Doyle of Melrose Park, Ill., to *AO*. This is

a corollary to *Weaver's Law*. It is sometimes referred to as *Doyle's Corollary*.)

● **Oeser's Law.** There is a tendency for the person in the most powerful position in an organization to spend all his time serving on committees and signing letters.
(*U/Co.*)

● **Office Holders, First Law of.** Get reelected.
(*U/Co.*)

● **Old Childrens' Law.** If it tastes good, you can't have it. If it tastes awful, you'd better clean your plate.
("The Wizard," FM 101, Youngstown, Ohio.)

● **O'Neill's Law of Time Saturation.** The news of the day, no matter how trivial or unimportant, always takes up more time than a married man has. *Corollary:* News stories expand and time contracts, meeting inexorably each day precisely twenty minutes after a man is supposed to be home for dinner.
(Named for Ray O'Neill, who was national affairs editor of *The New York Times*. It was explained in detail in an April 22, 1956, column by James Reston entitled "A Note to Miss Truman." Reston quotes Clifton Daniel as having told reporters that his hours at the *Times* were from 9:30 to 5:30. Countered Reston, "It is not a reporter's working hours that count, but the hours he works." He added, "These are regulated by the news and the news is regulated by a very simple mathematical rule." The rule, of course: *O'Neill's Law.*)

● **Oppenheimer's Observation.** The optimist thinks this is the best of all possible worlds, and the pessimist knows it.
(J. Robert Oppenheimer, in *The Bulletin of the Atomic Scientists,* February, 1951. *RS.*)

● **Optimum Optimorum Principle.** There comes a time when one must stop suggesting and evaluating new solutions, and get on with the job of analyzing and finally implementing one pretty good solution.

(Robert Machol, in his *POR* series. To illustrate the point of this principle, he points out that some years ago an ABM expert said that for optimal protection the entire continental United States could be covered with a mile-thick layer of peanut butter—it would be impenetrable and have the support of the peanut industry. Says Machol, "The point of this anecdote is that the solutions which may be suggested for a problem are inexhaustible.")

● **Orben's Packaging Discovery.** For the first time in history, one bag of groceries produces two bags of trash.

(Humorist Robert Orben. See also his *Travel, First Law of.*)

● **Orwell's Bridge Law.** All bridge hands are equally likely, but some are more equally likely than others.

(After George Orwell by Alan Truscott, in his *New York Times* bridge column for December 23, 1974.)

● **Osborn's Law.** Variables won't, constants aren't.

(Don Osborn, associate director, State of Arizona Solar Energy Commission. *S.T.L.*)

● **OSHA's Discovery.** Wet manure is slippery.

(The Occupational Health and Safety Administration [OSHA], in a finding reported in *The Washington Post* of June 18, 1976. This replaces an earlier U.S. Navy finding: "Classified material is considered lost when it cannot be found.")

● **O'Toole's Commentary on Murphy's Law.** Murphy was an optimist.

(Perhaps the most quoted of all the laws and corollaries to come in as a result of the *AO* columns, yet the name of the author or discoverer of the commentary is illegible. This unreadable signature could quickly lead to a situation in which O'Toole could raise as many questions as Murphy. Rumor has it that O'Toole was [a] a policeman in Newark during the riots and [b] a White House clerk during the last months of the Nixon Administration.)

● **Otten's Law of Testimony.** When a person says that in the interest of saving time, he will summarize his prepared statement, he will talk only three times as long as if he had read the statement in the first place.

● **Otten's Law of Typesetting.** Typesetters always correct intentional errors, but fail to correct unintentional ones.
(Both Alan Otten originals.)

● **Ozian Option.** I can't give you brains, but I can give you a diploma.
(The Wizard of Oz to the Scarecrow. *RS.*)

P

● **Paige's Six Rules for Life (Guaranteed to Bring Anyone to a Happy Old Age).** (1) Avoid fried foods which angry up the blood. (2) If your stomach disputes you, pacify it with cool thoughts. (3) Keep the juices flowing by jangling around gently as you move. (4) Go very lightly on the vices, such as carrying on in society, as the social ramble ain't restful. (5) Avoid running at all times. (6) Don't look back, something might be gaining on you.

(Baseball immortal Satchel Paige. *Co.*)

● **Panic Instruction for Industrial Engineers.** When you don't know what to do, walk fast and look worried.

(Bob Duckles, now with the Department of Commerce, picked this up from a plant engineer who had learned it at the Ford Motor Company.)

● **Paradox of Selective Equality.** All things being equal, all things are never equal.

(Marshall L. Smith.)

● **Pardee's Law.** There is an inverse relationship between the uniqueness of an observation and the number of investigators who report it simultaneously.

(A. B. Pardee, in his 1962 *American Scientist* article "pU, a New Quantity in Biochemistry." *FD.*)

● **Pardo's Postulates.** (1) Anything good is either illegal, immoral, or fattening. (2) The three faithful things in life are money, a dog, and an old woman. (3) Don't care if you're rich or not, as long as you can live comfortably and have everything you want.

(*U/S.T.L.*)

● **Pareto's Law. (The 20/80 Law.)** 20 percent of the customers account for 80 percent of the turnover, 20 percent of the components account for 80 percent of the cost, and so forth.

(After Vilfredo Pareto, the Italian economist [1848–1923]. *S.T.L.*)

Special Section 5

The Parkinson Contribution.

On November 19, 1955, an unsigned article appeared in *The Economist* simply entitled, "Parkinson's Law." As it was put in the first sentences:

> It is a commonplace observation that work expands so as to fill the time available for its completion. Thus, an elderly lady of leisure can spend the entire day in writing and dispatching a postcard to her niece at Bognor Regis. An hour will be spent in finding the postcard, another in hunting for spectacles, half an hour in search for the address . . .

The article went on to point out that the law came with two axiomatic additions that helped relate it to organizations:

Factor I—An official wants to multiply subordinates not rivals; and

Factor 2—Officials make work for each other.

In proving his contentions, the mysterious Parkinson showed, for example, that between 1914 and 1928 the number of ships in the Royal Navy went down by 67.74 percent, while the number of dockyard officials and clerks went up by 40.28 percent and Admiralty officials by a stunning 78.45 percent.

At first many thought that Parkinson was a fanciful name created by the magazine's editors. He was, in fact, C. Northcote Parkinson, a little-known history professor at the University of Malaya. Within a few years Parkinson became an international celebrity. His book was a best seller on both sides of the Atlantic and found its way into fourteen languages. He became an immensely popular lecturer, visiting professor, and essayist who occasionally added another law to his collection. As *Dun's Review* summed it up in a 1975 article on him, ". . . Parkinson has made a lucrative twenty-seven year career out of [a few] seemingly simple words."

Parkinson, who now lives on the island of Guernsey, has been asked many times why he thinks his law has had such an impact and seems to be as well used and widely quoted today as it was when it was newly coined. He always responds by saying that the main reason is that the law is true. He told *Dun's Review*, "[It] is as valid today as it was twenty years ago, because as a rule of nature it is immutable."

Here is a documented collection of Parkinson's laws:

1. *Parkinson's First Law*. Work expands so as to fill the time available for its completion.

2. *Parkinson's Second Law*. Expenditure rises to meet income.

3. *Parkinson's Third Law*. Expansion means complexity and complexity, decay; or to put it even more plainly—the more complex, the sooner dead.

4. *Parkinson's Law of Delay*. Delay is the deadliest form of denial.

5. *Parkinson's Law of Medical Research*. Successful re-

search attracts the bigger grant which makes further research impossible.

6. *Mrs. Parkinson's Law.* Heat produced by pressure expands to fill the mind available from which it can pass only to a cooler mind.

7. *Parkinson's New Law.* The printed word expands to fill the space available for it.

8. *Parkinson's Principle of Non-Origination.* It is the essence of grantsmanship to persuade the Foundation executives that it was *they* who suggested the research project and that you were a belated convert, agreeing reluctantly to all they had proposed.

9. *Parkinson's Finding on Journals.* The progress of science varies inversely with the number of journals published.

10. *Parkinson's Telephone Law.* The effectiveness of a telephone conversation is in inverse proportion to the time spent on it.

11. *Parkinson's Law of 1000.* An enterprise employing more than 1000 people becomes a self-perpetuating empire, creating so much internal work that it no longer needs any contact with the outside world.

The Parkinson contribution is twofold. First, his law, which is not only noteworthy when an institution shows that it is an exception to it rather than an example of it. A few years ago Anthony Lewis wrote in *The New York Times* that the Supreme Court "alone" among the great institutions did not

1. Book of the same title, Houghton Mifflin, Boston, 1957. 2. Essay of same title from *The Law and the Profits,* Houghton Mifflin, 1960. 3. Essay of same title from *In-Laws and Outlaws,* Houghton Mifflin, 1962. 4. Book of the same title, Houghton Mifflin, 1971. 5. Article of same title, *New Scientist,* 13:193 (1962.) 6. Book of the same title, Houghton Mifflin 1968. 7. Article of same title, *Reader's Digest,* February, 1963. 8. Same source as number 5. 9. *JIR,* Vol. 11/2. 10. Article of same title, *New York Times Magazine,* April 12, 1974. 11. This appears in various locations, including direct quotes from Parkinson that appear in F. P. Adler's "Relationship between Organization Size and Efficiency," *Management Science Journal,* October, 1960. Parkinson also told Adler, "With a research establishment the same point is reached but only after the staff is double that size" (i.e. 2000).

conform to the law. At the end of 1976, *Newsweek* asked if Jimmy Carter could repeal the law during his administration. At this writing, nothing has happened to indicate that he has. Second, Parkinson more than anyone else helped break the stranglehold of the pure sciences and mathematics on immutable laws, principles, and named effects. He paved the way for others and created an atmosphere in which an explanation like this could appear in *The Manchester Guardian:* ". . . much blame must attach itself to the [U.N.] administrative system, which has not only set out to prove Parkinson's Law, but which religiously follows the Peter Principle of promoting mediocrities."*

● **Parliament, Simple Rules for Interpreting Acts of.** Always avoid reading the preamble, which is likely to confuse rather than to enlighten. It sets forth not what the act is to do, but what it undoes, and confuses you with what the law was instead of telling you what it is to be.

When you come to a very long clause, skip it altogether, for it is sure to be unintelligible. If you try to attach one meaning to it, the lawyers are sure to attach another; and, therefore, if you are desirous of obeying an act of Parliament, it will be safer not to look at it, but wait until a few contrary decisions have been come to, and then act upon the latest.

When any clause says either one thing or the other shall be right, you may be sure that both will be wrong.

> (This comes from an old British Comic Almanac and appears in the anthology *Comic Almanac,* edited by Thomas Yoseloff, published by A. S. Barnes and Co., New York, 1963.)

*Hella Pick, *The Manchester Guardian Weekly,* July 25, 1970.

● **Parsons's Laws.** ■If you break a cup or plate, it will not be the one that was already chipped or cracked. ■A place you want to get to is always just off the edge of the map you happen to have handy. ■A meeting lasts at least 1½ hours however short the agenda. ■A piece of electronic equipment is housed in a beautifully designed cabinet, and at the side or on top is a little box containing the components which the designer forgot to make room for.

(Denys Parsons, London.)

● **Pastore's Comment on Michehls's Theorem.** Nothing is ultimate.

● **Pastore's Truths.** (1) Even paranoids have enemies. (2) This job is marginally better than daytime TV. (3) On alcohol: four is one more than more than enough.

(Jim Pastore, former Control Data Corp. manager. *S.T.L.*)

● **Patrick's Theorem.** If the experiment works, you must be using the wrong equipment.

(*U/ Scientific Collections.*)

● **Paturi Principle.** Success is the result of behavior that completely contradicts the usual expectations about the behavior of a successful person. *Reciprocity Theorem:* The amount of success is in inverse proportion to the effort in attaining success.

(Felix R. Paturi, pseudonym for a successful management engineer, who explains his principle and other theories in *The Escalator Effect,* Peter H. Weyden, 1973. The book contains many examples of the principle in operation. Here is just one: a small child who needs to get home quickly begins walking slower. He eventually stops and makes the "inaccurate and therefore inverse statement, 'I just can't anymore.' So then daddy carries him home.")

● **Paul Principle.** People become progressively less competent for jobs they once were well equipped to handle.

(Paul Armer, director of Stanford University's Computation Center, who first described it for a large audience in the June, 1970, issue of *The Futurist.* Armer is very concerned with the occupational hazard of "technological obsolesence" and argues for educational sabbaticals and other forms of continuing education. It was written, in part, in response to the *Peter Principle.*)

● **Peers's Law.** The solution to a problem changes the problem.

(John Peers, president, Logical Machine Corp. [LOMAC.])

● **Perelman's Point.** There is nothing like a good painstaking survey full of decimal points and guarded generalizations to put a glaze like a Sung vase on your eyeball.

(S. J. Perelman, quoted in *RS*'s *1974 Expectation of Days.*)

● **Perversity of Nature, Law of the (aka Mrs. Murphy's Corollary).** You cannot successfully determine beforehand which side of the bread to butter.

(*Co.*)

● **Perversity of Production Precept.** If it works well, they'll stop making it.

(*AO* credits Jane Otten and Russell Baker for this law. See also *Herblock's Law,* which it is close to.)

● **Peter Principle, Corollaries, Inversion, etc.** *Peter Principle:* In every hierarchy, whether it be government or business, each employee tends to rise to his level of incompetence; every post tends to be filled by an employee incompetent to execute its duties. *Corollaries:* (1) Incompetence knows no barriers of

time or place. (2) Work is accomplished by those employees who have not yet reached their level of incompetence. (3) If at first you don't succeed, try something else. *Peter's Inversion:* Internal consistency is valued more highly than efficiency. *Peter's Law:* The unexpected always happens. *Peter's Paradox:* Employees in a hierarchy do not really object to incompetence in their colleagues. *Peter's Placebo:* An ounce of image is worth a pound of performance. *Peter's Theorem:* Incompetence plus incompetence equals incompetence.

(Dr. Laurence J. Peter and Peter Hull, from their *The Peter Principle,* William Morrow and Co., 1969, with the exception of *Peter's Law,* which is from *PQ.* The *Peter Principle* ranks with *Parkinson's Law* and *Murphy's Law* as one of the most famous and widely applied laws of modern life. The *Peter Principle* is not without its critics, as others have attempted to revise or amend it [see, for instance, the *Paul Principle*], and no less an authority than Parkinson has remarked that it does not always work out in real life. Parkinson says that we get on an airplane with a fairly high level of confidence that the pilot and navigator will be able to find their destination. He concluded, however, that Peter had a right to make the conclusion that he did since he had spent his life in an area where the principle is literally true—institutions of higher education.)

● **Peterson's Law.** History shows that money will multiply in volume and divide in value over the long run. Or expressed differently, the purchasing power of currency will vary inversely with the magnitude of the public debt.

(Economist William H. Peterson, from his article in the November, 1959, issue of *Challenge.*)

● **Phases of a Project.**
1. Exultation.
2. Disenchantment.

3. Confusion.
4. Search for the Guilty.
5. Punishment of the Innocent.
6. Distinction for the Uninvolved.
(Project manager's wall poster, Battelle Memorial Institute, Columbus, Ohio.)

● **Phelps's Laws of Renovation.** (1) Any renovation project on an old house will cost twice as much and take three times as long as originally estimated. (2) Any plumbing pipes you choose to replace during renovation will prove to be in excellent condition; those you decide to leave in place will be rotten.
(Lew Phelps, Chicago. *AO.*)

● **Phelps's Law of Retributive Statistics.** An unexpectedly easy-to-handle sequence of events will be immediately followed by an equally long sequence of trouble.
(Charles Phelps, RAND Corp. economist. *AO.*)

● **Pierson's Law.** If you're coasting, you're going downhill.
(L. R. Pierson, from *Rumsfeld's Rules.*)

● **Pike's Law of Punditry.** Success provides more opportunities to say things than the number of things the pundit has worth saying.
(Writer and radio commentator Douglas Pike, Washington, D.C. Pike is an up-and-coming pundit whose producer understands the law and only lets him air his opinions once or twice every two weeks.)

● **Pipe, Axiom of the (aka Trischmann's Paradox).** A pipe gives a wise man time to think and a fool something to stick in his mouth.
(*Ed Trischmann/S.T.L.*)

● **Plotnick's Third Law.** The time of departure will be delayed by the square of the number of people involved. Simply stated, if I wish to leave the city at 5 P.M., I will most likely depart at 5:01. If I am to meet a friend, the time of departure becomes 5:04. If we were to meet another couple, we won't be on our way before 5:16, and so on.

    (Paul D. Plotnick, Stamford, Conn., in a letter to *The New York Times,* April 7, 1968. *FD.*)

● **Politicians' Rules.** (1) When the polls are in your favor, flaunt them. (2) When the polls are overwhelmingly unfavorable, (a) ridicule and dismiss them or (b) stress the volatility of public opinion. (3) When the polls are slightly unfavorable, play for sympathy as a struggling underdog. (4) When too close to call, be surprised at your own strength.

    (*U/JW.*)

● **Potter's Law.** The amount of flak received on any subject is inversely proportional to the subject's true value.

    (*U/S.T.L.*)

● **Powell's Law. [A.C.]** Never tell them what you wouldn't do.

    (Adam Clayton Powell, cited by Julian Bond in a radio interview.)

● **Powell's Laws. [J.]** (1) Bad news does not improve with age. *Corollary:* When in doubt, get it out. (2) [For handling professional baiters at daily briefings and other appropriate problems of life.] Indifference is the only sure defense.

    (Jody Powell, President Carter's press secretary.)

● **Pratt, The Rules of.** (1) If an apparently severe problem manifests itself, no solution is acceptable unless it is involved, expensive, and time-consuming. (2)(a) Completion of any task within the allocated time and budget does not bring credit upon the performing personnel—it merely proves the task was easier than expected; (b) failure to complete any task within the allocated time and budget proves the task was more difficult than expected and requires promotion for those in charge. (3) Sufficient monies to do the job correctly the first time are usually not available; however, ample funds are much more easily obtained for repeated major redesigns.

(From an undated clipping from *IEEE Spectrum*.)

● **Price's Law of Politics.** It's easier to be a liberal a long way from home.

(Don Price, dean of Harvard's Graduate School of Government, who discovered this when working with foundations that were more willing to undertake controversial projects overseas than in the United States. *AO*.)

● **Price's Law of Science.** Scientists who dislike the restraints of highly organized research like to remark that a truly great research worker needs only three pieces of equipment: a pencil, a piece of paper, and a brain. . . . But they quote this maxim more often at academic banquets than at budget hearings.

(Don Price. *RS*'s *1978 Expectation of Days.*)

● **Probable Dispersal, Law of.** Whatever hits the fan will not be evenly distributed. (Sometimes called *The How Come It All Landed on Me Law.*)

(Logical Machine Corp. ad, *The New Yorker,* 1976.)

● **Professional's Law.** Doctors, dentists, and lawyers are only on time for appointments when you're not.

(Rozanne Weissman.)

● **Professor Gordon's Rule of Evolving Bryographic Systems.** While bryographic plants are typically encountered in substrata of earthly or mineral matter in concreted state, discrete substrata elements occasionally display a roughly spherical configuration which, in presence of suitable gravitational and other effects, lends itself to combined translatory and rotational motion. One notices in such cases an absence of the otherwise typical accretion of bryophyta. We therefore conclude that a rolling stone gathers no moss.

(*U/ S.T.L.*)

● **Proverbial Law.** For every proverb that so confidently asserts its little bit of wisdom, there is usually an equal and opposite proverb that contradicts it.

(Writer Richard Boston in a review of *The Oxford Dictionary of English Proverbs* which appeared in *The New Statesman* for October 9, 1970. "Though many hands make light work, too many cooks spoil the broth," is just one example of Boston's discovery.)

● **Public Relations, Prime Rules of Political.** (1) Experts do not like surprises. It makes them look bad at the home office (e.g., JFK picking LBJ, Nixon picking Agnew, Reagan picking Schweiker). (2) Never say maybe in the same circulation area where you just said never.

(Both Vic Gold, from his *P.R. as in President.* The second was written relative to candidate Jimmy Carter saying no embargoes on grain shipments at the Iowa State Fair and then telling newspaper editors in Des Moines that he would make exceptions in times of national emergency.)

● **Public Relations Client Turnover Law.** The minute you sign a client is the minute you start to lose him.

(James L. Blankenship, senior vice-president, the public relations firm of R. C. Auletta and Co. Inc., New York.)

● **Public Speaking, First Rule of.** Nice guys finish fast.

(*Reader's Digest,* June, 1976.)

● **Pudder's Law.** Anything that begins well ends badly. Anything that begins badly ends worse.

(*U/S.T.L.*)

● **Purina Paradox.** You don't need to fly to have more fun with wings.

(Writer Joe Anderson discovered this law when he covered a story for *The Daily Oklahoman* in 1949. Let him explain: "In the late forties, a midwestern university and a manufacturer of chicken feed collaborated in breeding a wingless chicken which would prove meatier and more tender because it didn't flop around as much. It has never reached the market, however, because a rooster uses his wings to balance himself while in the process of impregnating a hen.")

● **Putney's Law.** If the people of a democracy are allowed to do so, they will vote away the freedoms which are essential to that democracy.

(Snell Putney in *The Conquest of Society,* Wadsworth Publishing, 1972. *JW.*)

R

● **Rakove's Laws of Politics.** (1) The amount of effort put into a campaign by a worker expands in proportion to the personal benefits that he will derive from his party's victory. (2) The citizen is influenced by principle in direct proportion to his distance from the political situation.

> (Milton Rakove of the University of Illinois, who first spelled them out in *The Virginia Quarterly Review*, Summer, 1965. *FL.*)

● **Randolph's Cardinal Principle of Statecraft.** Never needlessly disturb a thing at rest.

> (Early American statesman John Randolph of Richmond. Cited in a recent column by James J. Kilpatrick.)

● **Rapoport's Rule of the Roller-Skate Key.** Certain items which are crucial to a given activity will show up with uncommon regularity until the day when that activity is planned, at which point the item in question will disappear from the face of the earth.

> (Dan Rapoport, Washington writer.)

● **Raskin's Zero Law.** The more zeros found in the price tag for a government program, the less Congressional scrutiny it will receive.

> (Marcus Raskin, the Institute for Policy Studies, Washington, D.C. Collected by Barbara Raskin, novelist.)

● **Raspberry Jam, Law of.** The wider any culture is spread, the thinner it gets.

(Stanley Edgar Hyman. This was incorrectly attributed to Alvin Toffler in a *New York Times* article, which in turn gave birth to *Toffler's Law of Editorial Correction* [See *Editorial Correction, Law of*]. Toffler had reason to dispute it, as he had spent fourteen chapters of his book *The Culture Consumers* arguing that the *Law of Raspberry Jam* was wrong.)

● **Rather's Rule.** In dealing with the press do yourself a favor. Stick with one of three responses: (a) I know and I can tell you. (b) I know and I can't tell you, or (c) I don't know.
(Dan Rather, CBS. These were originally stated some years ago and appear in a collection of rules put together by Donald Rumsfeld.)

● **Rayburn's Rule.** If you want to get along, go along.
(House Speaker Sam Rayburn. *Co.*)

● **Rebecca's House Rules—** At Least One Fits Any Occasion.
1. Throw it on the bed.
2. Fry onions.
3. Call Jenny's mother.
4. No one's got the corner on suffering.
5. Run it under the cold tap.
6. Everything takes practice, except being born.
(Sharon Mathews, Arlington, Va.)

● **Reform, Fundamental Tenet of.** Reforms come from below. No man with four aces howls for a new deal.
(John F. Parker, *If Elected, I Promise,* Doubleday, 1960)

● **Restaurant Acoustics, Law of.** In a restaurant with seats which are close to each other, one will always find the decibel level of the nearest conversation to be inversely proportional to the quality of the thought going into it.

(Stuart A. Cohn. *AO.*)

● **Richman's Inevitables of Parenthood.** (1) Enough is never enough. (2) The sun always rises in the baby's bedroom window. (3) Birthday parties always end in tears. (4) Whenever you decide to take the kids home, it is always five minutes earlier that they break into fights, tears, hysteria.

(Phyllis C. Richman, writer and restaurant critic for *The Washington Post.*)

● **Riddle's Constant.** There are coexisting elements in frustration phenomena which separate expected results from achieved results.

(*U/Scientific Collections.*)

● **Riesman's Law.** An inexorable upward movement leads administrators to higher salaries and narrower spans of control.

(David Riesman. *JW.*)

● **Riggs's Hypothesis.** Incompetence tends to increase with the level of work performed. And, naturally, the individual's staff needs will increase as his level of incompetence increases.

(Arthur J. Riggs, in his article "Parkinson's Law, the Peter Principle, and the Riggs Hypothesis—A Synthesis," from the *Michigan Business Review,* March 1971. Riggs gives much detail on how his hypothesis fits in with the other principles in the title of his article. He also suggests a typical Riggs progression: ". . . from competent line worker to slightly incompetent foreman to incompetent supervisor." *FD.*)

● **Road Construction, Law of.** After large expenditures of federal, state, and county funds; after much confusion generated by detours and road blocks; after greatly annoying the surrounding population with noise, dust, and fumes, the previously existing traffic jam is relocated by one-half mile.

> (Alan Deitz, American Newspaper Publishers Association. *AO.*)

● **Robertson's Law.** Everything happens at the same time with nothing in between.

> (*U.* From Paul Hebig, Chicago, who adds, "It usually refers to social engagements and business meetings.")

● **Robotics, The Three Laws of.** (1) A robot may not injure a human being or, through inaction, allow a human being to come to harm. (2) A robot must obey the orders given it by human beings except where such orders would conflict with the First Law. (3) A robot must protect its own existence as long as such protection does not conflict with the First or Second.

> (Isaac Asimov, from "The Handbook of Robotics, 56th Edition, 2058 AD," which appears in his *I, Robot,* Doubleday, 1950.)

● **Rodovic's Rule.** In any organization, the potential is much greater for the subordinate to manage his superior than for the superior to manage his subordinate.

> (*U//JW.*)

● **Roemer's Law.** The rate of hospital admissions responds to bed availability. Or, If we insist on installing more beds, they will tend to get filled.

> (Dr. Milton Roemer of UCLA, who first suggested it in 1959. It is an entirely serious statement which, according to Victor R. Fuchs in his book *Who Shall Live?*, Basic Books, 1974, ". . . has received considerable support in recent econometric studies." *RS.*)

● **Rogers's Ratio.** One-third of the people in the United States promote, while the other two-thirds provide.
   (Will Rogers, quoted in Leonard C. Lewin's *Treasury of American Political Humor,* Dial, 1964.)

● **Rosenbaum's Rule.** The easiest way to find something lost around the house is to buy a replacement.
   (Jack Rosenbaum, in the *San Francisco Examiner and Chronicle.*)

● **Rosenstock-Huessy's Law of Technology.** All technology expands the space, contracts the time, and destroys the working group.
   (Eugen Rosenstock-Huessy, the German-American social philosopher and historian.)

● **Ross's Law. [A.]** Bare feet magnetize sharp metal objects so they always point upward from the floor—especially in the dark.
   (Al Ross. *JW.*)

● **Ross's Law. [C.]** Never characterize the importance of a statement in advance.
   (Charles G. Ross, President Truman's press secretary. This, along with *Hagerty's* and *Salinger's* laws, was collected by Robert Donovan of the *Los Angeles Times* a number of years ago. They have appeared in a number of places, including *FL* and *S.T.L.*)

● **Ross's Law of Public Transportation. [S.]** Scheduled changes always mean cutbacks. *Corollary:* Minor schedule adjustments always affect your bus (train, whatever).
   (Steve Ross, editor, *New Engineer.*)

● **Rowe's Rule.** The odds are 6 to 5 that the light at the end of the tunnel is a headlight of an oncoming express train.
(*U/"LSP."*)

● **Rudin's Law.** In a crisis that forces a choice to be made among alternative courses of action, most people will choose the worst one possible.
(S. A. Rudin of Atlanta, from a 1961 letter to *The New Republic. FL.*)

● **Rumsfeld's Rules** (A Sampling). ■ *On Serving the President:* Don't play President—you're not. The Constitution provides for only one President. Don't forget it and don't be seen by others as not understanding that fact. Where possible, preserve the President's options—he will very likely need them. Never say "The White House wants"—buildings don't "want." Don't speak ill of your predecessors (or successors)—you did not walk in their shoes. ■ *On Keeping Your Bearings in the White House:* Keep your sense of humor about your position. Remember the observation (attributed to General Joe Stilwell) that "the higher a monkey climbs, the more you see of his behind"—you will find that it has more than a touch of truth. Don't begin to believe you are indispensible or infallible, and don't let the President, or others, think you are—you're not. It's that simple. Don't forget that the fifty or so invitations you receive a week are sent not because those people are just dying to see you, but because of the position you hold. If you don't believe me, ask one of your predecessors how fast they stop. If you are lost—"Climb, conserve, and confess." (From the SNJ Flight Manual, as I recall from my days as a student naval aviator.) ■ *On Doing the Job in the White House:* Read and listen for what is missing. Many advisors —in and out of government—are quite capable of telling the President how to improve what has been proposed, or what's gone wrong. Few seem capable of sensing what isn't there. ■ *On Serving in Government:* When an idea is being pushed because it is "exciting," "new," or "innovative"—beware. An exciting, new, innovative idea can also be foolish. If in doubt, don't. If in doubt, do what is right. Your best question is often, "Why?" ■*On Politics, the Congress, and the Press:* The First Rule of Politics: You can't win unless you are on the ballot. Politics is human beings. Politics is addition, not subtraction. When someone with a rural accent says, "I don't know anything about politics," zip up your pockets. If you try to please everybody, somebody is not going to like it. With the press, it is safest to assume that there is no "off the record." ■*On Life (and other things):* It takes everyone to make a happy day. (Marcy Kay Rumsfeld at age seven.) In unanimity there may well be either cowardice or uncritical thinking. ■If you develop rules, never have more than ten.

> (Donald Rumsfeld, from the rules and observations he created and collected while at the Pentagon and White House. The rules here were excerpted from an article in the February, 1977, *Washingtonian* entitled "Rumsfeld's Rules." The article, in turn, was excerpted from Rumsfeld's original eighteen-page memo on rules.)

● **Runyon's Law.** The race is not always to the swift, nor the battle to the strong, but that's the way to bet.
(Damon Runyon. *PQ.*)

● **Rural Mechanics, First Rule of.** If it works, don't fix it.
(From William O'Neill, the National Geographic Society News Service.)

● **Russell's Observation.** In America everybody is of the opinion that he has no social superiors, since all men are equal, but he does not admit that he has no social inferiors, for, from the time of Jefferson onward, the doctrine that all men are equal applies only upwards, not downwards.

(Bertrand Russell, *Unpopular Essays,* Simon and Schuster, 1951. *RS.*)

● **Ryan's Law.** Make three correct guesses consecutively and you will establish yourself as an expert.
(*U/RS.*)

S

● **Sadat's Reminder.** Those who invented the law of supply and demand have no right to complain when this law works against their interest.

    (Anwar Sadat, quoted in *1978 Expectation of Days. RS.*)

● **Salinger's Law.** Quit when you're still behind.
(Pierre Salinger, President Kennedy's press secretary. He discovered it when he protested news reports that a lavish reception the President had held was "expensive." *FL.*)

● **Sam's Axioms.** (1) Any line, however short, is still too long. (2) Work is the crabgrass of life, but money is the water that keeps it green.

    (*U/S.T.L.*)

● **Sattingler's Law.** It works better if you plug it in.
(*U/Scientific Collections.*)

● **Sattler's Law.** There are 32 points to the compass, meaning that there are 32 directions in which a spoon can squirt grapefruit; yet, the juice almost invariably flies straight into the human eye.

    (Professor Louis Sattler, whose discovery appears in H. Allen Smith's *A Short History of Fingers* in the important essay "Fetridge's Law Explained.")

● **Saunders's Discovery.** Laziness is the mother of nine inventions out of ten.

    (Millionaire inventor Philip K. Saunders, quoted by Bennett Cerf in his *Laugh Day,* Doubleday, 1965.)

● **Sayre's Third Law of Politics.** Academic politics is the most vicious and bitter form of politics, because the stakes are so low.

> (The late Wallace Sayre of Columbia University has been given credit for this. A later corollary states: "They're the most vicious form of politics because the fighting is over issues decided five years earlier." *AO.*)

● **Schenk's First Principle of Industrial Market Economics.** Good salesmen and good repairmen will never go hungry.
> (Economist Robert E. Schenk, St. Joseph's College, Rensselaer, Ind. *AO.*)

● **Schickel's TV Theorems.** (1) Any dramatic series the producers want us to take seriously as a representation of contemporary reality cannot be taken seriously as a representation of anything—except a show to be ignored by anyone capable of sitting upright in a chair and chewing gum simultaneously. (2) The only programs a grown-up can possibly stand are those intended for children. Or, more properly, those that cater to those pre-adolescent fantasies that most have never abandoned.
> (Richard Schickel, from his review of the new television season, *Time,* September 22, 1975.)

● **Schuckit's Law.** All interference in human conduct has the potential for causing harm—no matter how innocuous the procedure may be.
> (Schuckit would appear to be a pseudonym. Collected by William K. Wright, San Diego, Cal.)

● **Schultze's Law.** If you can't measure output, then you measure input.
> (Charles Schultze as chairman, Council of Economic Advisors. *JW.*)

● **Schumpeter's Observation of Scientific and Non-scientific Theories.** Any theory can be made to fit any facts by means of appropriate additional assumptions.

> (Submitted by Schenk, of *Schenk's First Principle* . . . above. *AO.*)

● **Science, Two Important Observations from the Collection of Robert D. Specht.** (1) Science is a wonderful thing, but it has not succeeded in maximizing pleasure and minimizing pain, and that's all we asked of it. (2) A stagnant science is at a standstill.

> (The first comes from an unsigned "Notes and Comment" item in the June 13, 1970, issue of *The New Yorker.* The second is from *JIR,* December, 1973.)

● **Scientific Productivity of a Laboratory, Law of.**

$$\text{Productivity} = \frac{\text{Number of Secretaries} \times \text{Average Typing Speed}}{\text{Number of Scientists}}$$

> (From Robert Sommer's *Expertland,* Doubleday, 1963. He explains, "One interesting feature of this equation is that when the number of scientists is zero, productivity becomes infinite.")

● **Screwdriver Syndrome.** Sometimes, where a complex problem can be illuminated by many tools, one can be forgiven for applying the one he knows best.

> (Robert Machol, from his *POR.* It is illuminated by an anecdote in which an operations researcher is at home for the weekend with nothing to do and decides to tighten all the loose screws in the house. When he runs out of screws to tighten, he gets a file and begins filing slots in the heads of nails, which he dutifully begins tightening.)

● **Scriptural Injunctions and Observations** (A Sample). Old Scottish Prayer: O Lord, grant that we may always be right, For Thou knowest we will never change our minds.

 (JE.)

● **Second-Ratedness, Unfailing Law of.** Never be first to do anything.

 (Ken S., Wayland, Mass., in Ann Landers's column, 1978.)

● **Security Office, Special Law of.** Threats to security will be found. *Or, as an Axiom:* The finding of threats to security by a security office is totally predictable, and hence the finding is totally worthless.

 (Robert N. Kharasch in *The Institutional Imperative,* Charterhouse Books, 1973. *AO.*)

● **Segal's Law.** A man with one watch knows what time it is; a man with two watches is never sure.

 (U/S.T.L.)

● **Selective Gravity, Law of.** An object will fall so as to do the most damage. *Jennings's Corollary:* The chance of the bread falling buttered side down is directly proportional to the cost of the carpet.

 (The law is common on scientific lists. The corollary was first spotted in a list by Arthur Bloch, "18 Unnatural Laws," which appears in the best-selling *Book of Lists* by David Wallechinsky, Irving Wallace, and Amy Wallace.)

● **Sells's Law.** The first sample is always the best.
 (U. From William K. Wright.)

● **Serendipity, Laws of.** (1) In order to discover anything you must be looking for something. (2) If you wish to make an improved product, you must already be engaged in making an inferior one.

(These come from William K. Wright's collection. He attributes the first to Harvey Neville and the second to Jacob A. Varela.)

● **Sevareid's Law.** The chief cause of problems is solutions. (Eric Sevareid, on the CBS *News* for December 29, 1970.)

● **Shaffer's Law.** The effectiveness of a politician varies in inverse proportion to his commitment to principle.
(Newsweek reporter Sam Shaffer. *JW.)*

● **Shalit's Law.** The intensity of movie publicity is in inverse ratio to the quality of the movie.
(Gene Shalit, *The Today Show. S.T.L.*)

● **Shanahan's Law.** The length of a meeting rises with the square of the number of people present.
(Eileen Shanahan, when economics reporter for *The New York Times. FL.*)

● **Sharkey's 4th Law of Motion.** Passengers on elevators constantly rearrange their positions as people get on and off so there is at all times an equal distance between all bodies.
(John Sharkey of *The Washington Post.*)

● **Shaw's Principle.** Build a system that even a fool can use, and only a fool will want to use it.
(Christopher J. Shaw. *JE.*)

● **Shelton's Laws of Pocket Calculators.** (1) Rechargeable batteries die at the most critical time of the most complex problem. (2) When a rechargable battery starts to die in the middle of a complex calculation, and the user attempts to connect house current, the calculator will clear itself. (3) The final answer will exceed the magnitude or precision or both of the calculator. (4)

There are not enough storage registers to solve the problem. (5) The user will forget mathematics in proportion to the complexity of the calculator. (6) Thermal paper will run out before the calculation is complete.

(John L. Shelton, president, Sigma Beta Communications, Inc., Dallas.)

● **Short's Quotations** (Some of many). ■Any great truth can—and eventually will—be expressed as a cliché—a cliché is a sure and certain way to dilute an idea. For instance, my grandmother used to say, "The black cat is always the last one off the fence." I have no idea what she meant, but at one time, it was undoubtedly true. ■Half of being smart is knowing what you're dumb at. ■Malpractice makes malperfect. ■Neurosis is a communicable disease. ■The only winner in the War of 1812 was Tchaikovsky. ■Nature abhors a hero. For one thing, he violates the law of conservation of energy. For another, how can it be the survival of the fittest when the fittest keeps putting himself in situations where he is most likely to be creamed? ■A little ignorance can go a long way. ■Learn to be sincere. Even if you have to fake it. ■There is no such thing as an absolute truth—that is absolutely true. ■Understanding the laws of nature does not mean we are free from obeying them. ■Entropy has us outnumbered. ■The human race never solves any of its problems—it only outlives them. ■TINSTAFL!—There is no such thing as free love. ■Hell hath no fury like a pacifist.

(David Gerrold, from two of his 1978 columns in *Starlog*. They come from his "Quote-book of Solomon Short"—Short being a first-cousin to Robert A. Heinlein's Lazarus Long. [See *Long's Notes.*] He is also the author of *Gerrold's Three Laws of Infernal Dynamics.*)

● **Simmons's Law.** The desire for racial integration increases with the square of the distance from the actual event. (*U/J.W*)

● **Simon's Law.** Everything put together sooner or later falls apart.

(Paul Simon. *S.T.L.*)

● **Sinner's Law of Retaliation.** Do whatever your enemies don't want you to do.

(Gary Novak, Highmore, S. Da.)

● **Skinner's Constant.** That quantity which, when multiplied by, divided by, added to, or subtracted from the answer you get, gives you the answer you should have gotten.

(*U/AIC.* Sometimes known as *Flannegan's Finagling Factor. FD* says this was called *DeBunk's Universal Variable Constant* in the 1930s.)

● **Skole's Rule of Antique Dealers.** Never simply say, "Sorry, we don't have what you are looking for." Always say, "Too bad, I just sold one the other day."

(Robert Skole, reporter, Stockholm, Sweden.)

● **Slide Presentation, Law of.** In any slide presentation, at least one slide will be upside down or backwards, or both.

(John Corcoran, whose entry in the *Directory of Washington Independent Writers* reads, in part, "Send for clips to see how I write. If you don't, frogs will sneak into your house and eat your fingers.")

● **Smith's Laws of Politics and Other Things.** ■A politician always abuses his own constituency and placates the opponent's. ■The main beneficiaries of federal aid are those states that most oppose the principle. ■A baseball player who makes a spectacular defensive play always leads off the next inning as batter. ■A person over age 65 who drinks says that his doctor recommends it.

(Bob Smith, Washington, D.C., founder, editor, and publisher of *The Privacy Journal.*)

● **Smith's Principles of Bureaucratic Tinkertoys.** (1) Never use one word when a dozen will suffice. (2) If it can be understood, it's not finished yet. (3) Never do anything for the first time.

(*U.* From Paul Herbig, Chicago, Ill.)

● **Socio-Genetics, First Law of.** Celibacy is not hereditary. (Proposed by Guy Godin in *JIR* in 1975 and quickly questioned. Wrote one reader, "If your parents didn't have any children, the odds are that you won't have any.")

● **Sod's Law.** The degree of failure is in direct proportion to the effort expended and to the need for success.

(Generally speaking, Sod is the British incarnation of Finagle, Gumperson, Murphy, *et al.* One authority on Sod's Law is Richard Boston of London, who has written of it in such periodicals as *The New Statesman* and *The Times Literary Supplement.* Boston does not claim to be its author: on the contrary, he has traced a version of it back to a Lancashire proverb dating from 1871, "The bread never falls but on its buttered side." He also reports that in France it is called *La loi d'emmerdement maximum.*

However, Boston's greatest contribution may be in telling the story of the man whose bread fell and landed buttered side up. He ran straight away to his rabbi to report this deviance from one of the basic rules of the universe. At first the rabbi would not believe him but finally became convinced that it had happened. However, he didn't feel qualified to deal with the question and passed it along to one of world's leading Talmudic scholars. After months of waiting, the scholar finally came up with an answer: "The bread must have been buttered on the wrong side.")

● **Spare Parts Principle.** The accessibility, during recovery of small parts which fall from the work bench, varies directly with the size of the part—and inversely with its importance to the completion of the work underway.

(*AIC.*)

● **Specht's Meta-law.** Under any conditions, anywhere, whatever you are doing, there is some ordinance under which you can be booked.

(Robert D. Specht of the RAND Corp., who is also collector *R.S.*)

● **Spencer's (Contradictory) Corollary (to Nofziger's Law of Detail.** If a political candidate chooses to go into specifics on a program that affects a voter's self-interest, the voter *gets* interested. If the proposal involves money, he gets very interested.

(Stuart Spencer of President Ford's PR staff, *re* Reagan's proposed $90 billion cut in the federal budget. From Vic Gold's *P.R. as in President.*)

● **Sprague's Law.** Satisfaction derived from a trip goes down as Expectation goes up *if* Reality is unchanged $S = R/E$ As Reality becomes more favorable, the chance for Satisfaction goes up *if* Expectation is unchanged.

(Hall T. Sprague, *The New York Times,* Travel section, January 16, 1977. *JW.*)

● **Stamp's Statistical Probability.** The government [is] extremely fond of amassing great quantities of statistics. These are raised to the nth degree, the cube roots are extracted, and the results are arranged into elaborate and impressive displays. What must be kept ever in mind, however, is that in every case, the figures are first put down by a village watchman, and he puts down anything he damn well pleases.

(Attributed to Sir Josiah Stamp, 1840–1941, H.M. collector of inland revenue. From rules collected by Donald Rumsfeld.)

● **Steele's Plagiarism of Somebody's Philosophy.** Everyone should believe in something—I believe I'll have another drink.

(Mary Steele. *S.T.L.*)

● **Steinbeck's Law.** When you need towns, they are very far apart.

(John Steinbeck, on the occasion of coming down with car trouble on a lonely road in Oregon while researching *Travels with Charlie*. Recalled by H. Allen Smith in *A Short History of Fingers*.)

● **Stephens's Soliloquy.** Finality is death. Perfection is finality. Nothing is perfect. There are lumps in it.

(James Stephens, quoted in *The Public Speaker's Treasure Chest*.)

● **Stockbroker's Declaration.** The market will rally from this or lower levels.

(Larry W. Sisson, Seattle. *AO.*)

● **Stock Market Axiom.** The public is always wrong.
(*U/ Co.*)

● **Sturgeon's Law.** 90 percent of everything is crud.
(Science fiction writer Theodore Sturgeon. This law is widely quoted—from *The Washington Post* to *Harper's*

—with the percentages varying from 90 to 99 percent and the last word variously "crud" or "crap.")

● **Suhor's Law.** A little ambiguity never hurt anyone.
(Charles Suhor, deputy executive director, National Council of Teachers of English. He formulated the law when he discovered "the universe is intractably squiggly.")

● **Survival Formula for Public Office.** (1) Exploit the inevitable (which means, take credit for anything good which happens whether you had anything to do with it or not.) (2) Don't disturb the perimeter (meaning don't stir a mess unless you can be sure of the result.) (3) Stay in with the Outs (the Ins will make so many mistakes you can't afford to alienate the Outs.) (4) Don't permit yourself to get between a dog and a lampost.
(*AO.*)

● **Sutton's Law.** Go where the money is.
(Named after bank robber Willie Sutton who, when asked why he robbed banks replied, "Because that's where the money is." It is used regularly in a number of fields today where, when the question of which direction to take is asked, it is common to simply say "Let Sutton's Law apply." Machol uses it as one of his *Principles of Operations Research,* but it is also applied in fields as diverse as medical research and broadcasting.)

● **Swipple Rule of Order.** He who shouts loudest has the floor.
(*U/S.T.L.*)

● **Symington's Law.** For every credibility gap there is a gullibility gap.
(Senator Stuart Symington quoted in a recent Ann Landers column.)

T

- **Taxi Principle.** Find out the cost before you get in. (Posted in U.S. Department of Labor. *TO'B.*)

- **Technology, Law of.** The very technology that makes our living simpler makes society more complex. The more efficient we get, the more specialized we become and the more dependent.

  (Thomas Griffith, *The Waste-High Culture,* Harper & Row, 1959.)

- **Terman's Law of Innovation.** If you want a track team to win the high jump, you find one person who can jump seven feet, not seven people who can jump one foot.

  (Frederick E. Terman, provost emeritus, Stanford University. See also *Bowker's Law.*)

- **Thermopolitical Rhetoric, Laws of.** (1) Cant produces countercant. *Corollary:* The quantity of rhetoric has been directly proportional to the lack of action. (2) Social groups are generally in disarray. To protect themselves from other groups, especially the groups just below them, groups will attempt to convey an appearance of interior order and purpose they do not possess. (3) Social institutions will change only at the speed required to protect them from attack—slowly or fast to the degree required, but usually slowly. They will put off change as long as possible . . .

  (Arthur Herzog, from his book *The B. S. Factor: The Theory and Technique of Faking It in America,* Simon and Schuster, 1973.)

● **Third Corollary.** The difficulty of getting anything started increases with the square of the number of people involved.
(Jim MacGregor. *AO.*)

● **Thoreau's Law.** If you see a man approaching you with the obvious intent of doing you good, you should run for your life.
(Attributed to Thoreau by William H. Whyte, Jr., in *The Organization Man,* Simon and Schuster, 1956, and quoted in *MB, S.T.L.*, etc.)

● **Thoreau's Rule.** Any fool can make a rule, and every fool will mind it.
(Thoreau. *JW.*)

● **Thurber's Conclusion.** There is no safety in numbers, or in anything else.
(James Thurber, *Fables for Our Time*, Harper & Row, 1939. *RS.*)

● **Tipper's Law.** Those who expect the biggest tips provide the worst service.
(Rozanne Weissman.)

● **Tishbein's Law.** There are more horses' backsides in the military service of the United States than there are horses.
(*U.* Robert J. Clark of Southampton, N.Y., learned this as a plebe at West Point and passed it along to *AO.*)

● **Titanic Coincidence.** Most accidents in well-designed systems involve two or more events of low probability occurring in the worst possible combination.
(Robert Machol, in *POR.*)

● **Tom Jones's Law.** Friends may come and go, but enemies accumulate.

(Dr. Thomas Jones, president of the University of South Carolina.)

● **Tom Sawyer's Great Laws of Human Action.** (1) In order to make [a person] covet a thing, it is only necessary to make the thing difficult to attain. (2) Work consists of whatever a body is *obliged* to do, and Play consists of whatever a body is not obliged to do.
(Samuel Clemens, *Tom Sawyer.*)

● **Torquemada's Law.** When you are sure you're right, you have a moral duty to impose your will upon anyone who disagrees with you.
(Robert W. Mayer, Champaign, Ill. *AO.*)

● **Transcription Square Law.** The number of errors made is equal to the sum of the "squares" involved.
(*AIC.*)

● **Travel, First Law of.** No matter how many rooms there are in the motel, the fellow who starts up his car at five o'clock in the morning is always parked under your window.
(Comedy writer Bob Orben.)

● **Tribune Tower, Law of.** Elevators traveling in the desired direction are always delayed and on arrival tend to run in pairs, threes of a kind, full houses, etc.
(Pete Maiken, *The Chicago Tribune.*)

● **Truman's Law.** If you can't convince them, confuse them.
(Harry S Truman. *Co.*)

● **Truths of Management.** (1) Think before you act; it's not your money. (2) All good management is the expression of one great idea. (3) No executive devotes effort to proving himself wrong. (4) Cash in must exceed cash out. (5) Management capability is always less than the organization actually needs. (6) Either an executive can do his job or he can't. (7) If sophisticated calculations are needed to justify an action, don't do it. (8) If you are doing something wrong, you will do it badly. (9) If you are attempting the impossible, you will fail. (10) The easiest way of making money is to stop losing it.

> (Robert Heller, *The Great Executive Dream,* Delacorte, 1972. *JE.*)

● **Turner's Law.** Nearly all prophecies made in public are wrong.

> (Malcolm Turner, Scottish journalist, passed along to *AO* by his son Arthur Campbell Turner, a California political scientist.)

● **Twain's Rule.** Only kings, editors, and people with tapeworm have the right to use the editorial "we."
(Samuel Clemens. *Co.*)

● **Tylk's Law.** Assumption is the mother of all foul-ups.
(*U/"LSP"*)

U

● **Ubell's Law of Press Luncheons.** At any public relations luncheon, the quality of the food is inversely related to the quality of the information.

（Earl Ubell, who created it when he was the New York *Herald Tribune*'s science writer. Recalled by Ben Bagdikian.)

● **Uhlmann's Razor.** When stupidity is a sufficient explanation, there is no need to have recourse to any other. *Corollary:* (Also, the *Law of Historical Causation.*) "It seemed like the thing to do at the time."

(Michael M. Uhlmann, who was assistant attorney general for legislation in the Ford Administration. *AO* and *JMcC.*)

● **Ultimate Law.** All general statements are false.

(R. H. Grenier, Davenport, Iowa. *AO.*)

● **Ultimate Principle.** By definition, when you are investigating the unknown, you do not know what you will find.

(*Scientific Collections.*)

● **Umbrella Law.** You will need three umbrellas: one to leave at the office, one to leave at home, and one to leave on the train.

(James L. Blankenship, R. C. Auletta and Co., New York.)

● **United Law.** If an organization carries the word "united" in its name, it means it isn't, e.g., United Nations, United Arab Republic, United Kingdom, United States.

(Professor Charles I. Issawi, quoting Warner Schilling, professor of political science, who is quoting Professor Harry Rudin. From *Issawi's Laws of Social Motion*.)

● **Universal Field Theory of Perversity (or Mulé's Law).** The probability of an event's occurring varies directly with the perversity of the inanimate object involved and inversely with the product of its desirability and the effort expended to produce it.
（Walter Mulé, from his article "Beyomd Murphy's Law" in *Northliner*. Mulé uses his article as proof of the law, whereas if it had not appeared in print it would have been an example of *Murphy's Law*.)

● **Unnamed Law.** If it happens, it must be possible.
(*RS.*)

● **Unspeakable Law.** As soon as you mention something if it's good, it goes away. . . . If it's bad, it happens.
(From Bloch's list in *The Book of Lists*.)

V

● **Vail's First Axiom.** In any human enterprise, work seeks the lowest hierarchical level.

(Charles R. Vail, vice-president, Southern Methodist University.)

● **Vance's Rule of 2 ½.** Any military project will take twice as long as planned, cost twice as much, and produce only half of what is wanted.

(Attributed to Cyrus Vance when he was under secretary of defense. *AO.*)

● **Vique's Law.** A man without religion is like a fish without a bicycle.

(Semi-*U*. Conrad Schneiker believes Vique is a friend of Edith Folta's in Urbanna, Ill. Gregg Townsend is not sure of this. Nonetheless, it is a popular law that has begun to show up in variant forms, such as at a recent NOW conference, where several delegates were reported to have said, "A woman without a man . . ." etc.)

● **Von Braun's Law of Gravity.** We can lick gravity, but sometimes the paperwork is overwhelming.

(The late Wernher von Braun, during the early months of the U.S. space program.)

W

● **Waddell's Law of Equipment Failure.** A component's degree of reliability is directly proportional to its ease of accessibility (i.e., the harder it is to get to, the more often it breaks down.)

> (Johnathan Waddell, crew member, *Exxon New Orleans,* oil tanker.)

● **Waffle's Law.** A professor's enthusiasm for teaching the introductory course varies inversely with the likelihood of his having to do it.

> (*U.* Quoted in "The Geologic Column" in *Geotimes* for July-August, 1968. The author of the column is Robert L. Bates. *FD.*)

● **Wakefield's Refutation of the Iron Law of Distribution.** Them what gets—has.

> (Dexter B. Wakefield of Coral Gables, Fla., in a letter to *The Wall Street Journal,* November 11, 1974.)

● **Waldo's Observation.** One man's red tape is another man's system.

> (Dwight Waldo, from his essay "Government by Procedure," which appears in Fritz Morstein Marx's *Elements of Public Administration,* Prentice-Hall, 1946.)

● **Walinsky's Laws.** (1) The intelligence of any discussion diminishes with the square of the number of participants. (2) *His First Law of Political Campaigns:* If there are twelve clowns in a ring, you can jump in the middle and start reciting Shake-

W

182

speare, but to the audience, you'll just be the thirteenth clown.
(Adam Walinsky. *AO.*)

● **Walker's Law.** Associate with well-mannered persons and your manners will improve. Run with decent folk and your own decent instincts will be strengthened. Keep the company of bums and you will become a bum. Hang around with rich people and you will end by picking up the check and dying broke.
(Stanley Walker, city editor of the New York *Herald Tribune* during the 1930s. It was rediscovered by Alan Deitz of the American Newspaper Publishers Association, who passed it along to *AO* with this comment, "Although there are no facts to substantiate this, it was probably enunciated by Walker after spending an evening with Lucius Beebe and Ogden Reid in Jack Bleek's.)

● **Walters's Law of Management.** If you're already in a hole, there's no use to continue digging.
(Roy W. Walters, Roy Walters Associates, Glen Rock, N.J.)

● **Washington's Law.** Space expands to house the people to perform the work that Congress creates.
(Haynes Johnson, *The Washington Post,* August 14, 1977.)

● **Weaver's Law.** When several reporters share a cab on assignment, the reporter in the front seat pays for all.
(Named for Warren Weaver of *The New York Times.* See also *Doyle's Corollary* and *Germond's Law. AO.*)

● **Weidner's Queries.** (1) The tide comes in and the tide goes out, and what have you got? (2) They say an elephant never forgets, but what's he got to remember?
(*U.* From Dave Miliman, Baltimore, Maryland.)

● **Weight-Watcher's Law.** Better to throw it OUT—than throw it in.

> (Attributed to one Skinny Mitchell in a letter from "Benton Harbor Ben" from Ann Landers's column.)

● **Weiler's Law.** Nothing is impossible for the man who doesn't have to do it himself.

> (A. H. Weiler of *The New York Times. FL.*)

● **Weinberg's Law.** If builders built buildings the way programmers wrote programs, then the first woodpecker that came along would destroy civilization. *Corollary:* An expert is a person who avoids the small errors while sweeping on to the grand fallacy.

> (Gerald Weinberg, computer scientist, University of Nebraska. *JE.*)

● **Weisman's College Exam Law.** If you're confident after you've just finished an exam, it's because you don't know enough to know better.

> (Jay Weisman, Easton, Pa.)

● **Wells's Law.** A parade should have bands *or* horses, not both.

> (Nancy M. Wells, San Pedro [Cal.] High School teacher and representative at large to the National Council of Teachers of English.)

● **Westheimer's Rule.** To estimate the time it takes to do a task: estimate the time you think it should take, multiply by two, and change the unit of measure to the next highest unit. Thus we allocate two days for a one-hour task.

> (*U/S.T.L.*)

● **Whispered Rule.** People will believe anything if you whisper it.

> (*The Farmers' Almanac,* 1978 edition.)

● **White Flag Principle.** A military disaster may produce a better postwar situation than victory.

(Shimon Tzabar, in a book of the same title, Simon and Schuster, 1972. He says that if you can accept the principle, "then there can be a science of military disasters as there is a science of military victories." He adds, "Such a science must comprise a theory and a practice. The practice should provide the armies with handbooks and textbooks for the accomplishment of defeats and surrenders. The fact that the big powers of today are powerful enough to make absurd any effort by lesser powers to overcome them in the traditional way, makes an alternative to victory the more urgent.")

● **White's Statement.** Don't lose heart . . . (*Owen's Comment on White's Statement:* . . . they might want to cut it out . . . *Byrd's Addition to Owen's Comment on White's Statement:* . . . and they want to avoid a lengthy search.)
(*U/S.T.L.*)

● **Wicker's Law.** Government expands to absorb revenue —and then some.
(Tom Wicker, *The New York Times. FL.*)

● **Wilcox's Law.** A pat on the back is only a few centimeters from a kick in the pants.
(*U/RS.*)

● **Will's Rule of Informed Citizenship.** If you want to understand your government, don't begin by reading the Constitution. (It conveys precious little of the flavor of today's statecraft). Instead read selected portions of the Washington telephone directory containing listings for all the organizations with titles beginning with the word "National."
(George Will. *JW.*)

● **Wilson's Law of Demographics. [W.]** The public is not made up of people who get their names in the newspapers. (Woodrow Wilson. *MBC.*)

● **Wilson's Laws. [J.Q.]** (1) All policy interventions in social problems produce the intended effect—*if* the research is carried out by those implementing the policy or their friends. (2) No policy intervention in social problems produces the intended effect—*if* the research is carried out by independent third parties, especially those skeptical of the policy.
(James Q. Wilson, Harvard political scientist, in his article "On Pettigrew and Armor" in *Public Interest,* Winter, 1973.)

● **Wing-Walking, First Law of.** Never leave hold of what you've got until you've got hold of something else.
(Donald Herzberg, dean of Georgetown University's graduate school, reported to *AO.* It came from the days of the barnstorming pilots and is now applied in situations such as when one quits a job before having another lined up.)

● **Witzenburg's Law of Airplane Travel.** The distance between the ticket counter and your plane is directly proportional to the weight of what you are carrying and inversely proportional to the time remaining before takeoff.
(Gary Witzenburg, Troy, Mich.)

● **Wober's SNIDE Rule.** Ideal goals grow faster than the means of attaining new goals allow.
(Mallory Wober, *JIR,* March, 1971. The acronym SNIDE stands for Satisfied Needs Incite Demand Excesses.)

● **Wolf's Laws.** ■*Historical Lessons:* Those who don't study the past will repeat its errors. Those who do study it, will

find *other* ways to err! ■ *Decision-making:* Major actions are rarely decided by more than four people. If you think a larger meeting you're attending is really "hammering out" a decision, you're probably wrong. Either the decision was agreed to by a smaller group before the meeting began, or the outcome of the larger meeting will be modified later when three or four people get together. ■ *Briefings:* In briefings to busy people, summarize at the beginning what you're *going to tell* them, then *tell* them, then summarize at the end what you *have told* them. ■ *Good*

Management: The tasks to do immediately are the minor ones; otherwise, you'll forget them. The major ones are often better to defer. They usually need more time for reflection. Besides, if you forget them, they'll remind you. ■*Meetings:* The only important result of a meeting is agreement about next steps. ■*Planning:* A good place to start from is where you are. ■*Wolf's Law* (subtitled, *An Optimistic View of a Pessimistic World*)*:* It isn't that things will necessarily go wrong (*Murphy's Law*), but rather that they will take so much more time and effort than you think, if they are not to. ■*Tactics:* If you can't beat them, have them join you.

(Charles Wolf, Jr., head, economics department, the RAND Corp., and director, RAND Graduate Institute. *RS.* See also *Baldy's Law,* which is also Wolf's.)

● **Woman's Equation.** Whatever women do, they must do twice as well as men to be thought half as good. Luckily, this is not difficult.

(*U/RS.*)

● **Wood's Law.** The more unworkable the urban plan, the greater the probability of implementation.

(Robert Wood, *Ekistics,* October, 1969. *JW.*)

● **Woodward's Law.** A theory is better than its explanation.

(H. P. Woodward, in a letter to Robert L. Bates, who published it in his "Geologic Column" in the July-August, 1968, *Geotimes.*)

Special Section 6

Work Rules. (Found posted in various locations about the working world.)

> *RULES.*
>
> 1.   THE BOSS IS ALWAYS RIGHT.
> 2.   WHEN THE BOSS IS WRONG, REFER TO *RULE 1.*

> THE WORKER'S DILEMMA.
> 1. No matter how much you do, you'll never do enough.
> 2. What you don't do is always more important than what you do do.

> NEW WORK RULES.
>
> *Sickness.* No excuses will be acceptable. We will no longer accept your doctor's statement as proof of illness, as we believe that if you are able to go to the doctor, you are able to come to work.

Leave of Absence (for an Operation.) We are no longer allowing this practice. We wish to discourage any thoughts that you may need all of whatever you have, and you should not consider having something removed. We hired you as you are, and to have anything removed would certainly make you less than we bargained for.

Death (Other Than Your Own). This is no excuse. If you can arrange for funeral services to be held late in the afternoon, however, we can let you off an hour early, provided all your work is up to date.

Death (Your Own). This will be accepted as an excuse, but we would like at least two weeks' notice, as we feel it is your duty to teach someone else your job.

Also, entirely too much time is being spent in the washrooms. In the future, you will follow the practice of going in alphabetical order. For instance, those whose surnames begin with "A" will be allowed to go from 9–9:05 A.M., and so on. If you are unable to go at your appointed time, it will be necessary to wait until the next day when your time comes around again.

THE TWO KINDS OF WORK

Work is of two kinds: (1) Altering the position of matter at or near the earth's surface relative to other such matter; (2) Telling other people to do so.

The first is unpleasant and ill paid; the second is pleasant and highly paid.

—*The Rotarian.*

Eat a live toad the first thing in the morning and nothing worse will happen to you the rest of the day.

Our troops advanced today without losing a foot of ground.
——*Spanish Civil War Communiqué.*

Anyone can do any amount of work provided it isn't the work he is supposed to be doing at that moment.
——*Robert Benchley.*

ANNOUNCEMENT.

(These rules were printed in the *Boston Globe* some years ago and were reported to be the rules posted by the owner of a New England carriage works in 1872, as a guide to his office workers.)

1. Office employees will daily sweep the floors, dust the furniture, shelves, and showcases.

2. Each day fill lamps, clean chimneys, and trim wicks. Wash the windows once a week.

3. Each clerk will bring in a bucket of water and scuttle of coal for the day's business.

4. Make your pens carefully. You may whittle nibs to your individual taste.

5. This office will open at 7 A.M. and close at 8 P.M. except on the Sabbath, on which day we will remain closed. Each employee is expected to spend the Sabbath by attending church and contributing liberally to the cause of the Lord.

6. Men employees will be given off each week for courting purposes, or two evenings a week if they go regularly to church.

7. After an employee has spent his 13 hours of labor in the office, he should spend the remaining time reading the Bible and other good books.

8. Every employee should lay aside from each pay a goodly sum of his earnings for his benefit during his declining years, so that he will not become a burden on society or his betters.

9. Any employee who smokes Spanish cigars, uses liquor in any form, or frequents pool and public halls, or gets shaved in a barber shop, will give me good reason to suspect his worth, intentions, integrity and honesty.

10. The employee who has performed his labors faithfully and without a fault for five years, will be given an increase of five cents per day in his pay, providing profits from the business permit it.

● **Wynne's Law.** Negative slack tends to increase. (*U/S.T.L.*)

X

● **Xerces Englebraun's Big Man Syndrome.** The importance of the man and his job, in that relative order, rises in direct proportion to the distance separating his audience from his home office.

    (This Shanghai psychiatrist appears in *For Men With Yen* by Alan Rosenberg and William J. O'Neill, Wayward Press, Tokyo, 1962.)

Y

● **Yapp's Basic Fact.** If a thing cannot be fitted into something smaller than itself some dope will do it.

   (Eric Frank Russell, in a November, 1959, letter to *ASF*. Yapp discovered this fact at an early age when he got his head stuck in a fence and had to be freed by the fire department. *FD.*)

● **Yolen's Law of Self-Praise.** Proclaim yourself "World Champ" of something—tiddly-winks, rope-jumping, whatever—send this notice to newspapers, radio, TV, and wait for challengers to confront you. Avoid challenges as long as possible, but continue to send news of your achievements to all media. Also, develop a newsletter and letterhead for communications.

   (Will Yolen, former PR man and kite VIP, who by now probably owns a suitcase filled with clippings of articles that talk about him and his World Championship.)

Z

● **Zellar's Law.** Every newspaper, no matter how tight the news hole, has room for a story on another newspaper increasing its newsstand price.

(Ed Zellar, Park Ridge, Ill. *AO.*)

● **Zimmerman's Law.** Regardless of whether a mission expands or contracts, administrative overhead continues to grow at a steady rate.

("*LSP*" list, which identifies him as Charles J. Zimmerman. *C.L.U.*)

● **Zimmerman's Law of Complaints.** Nobody notices when things go right.

(M. Zimmerman. *AO.*)

● **Zusmann's Rule.** A successful symposium depends on the ratio of meeting to eating.

(*U.* From a group of "Quips" in the *JIR,* March, 1971.)

● **Zymurgy's First Law of Evolving System Dynamics.** Once you open a can of worms, the only way to recan them is to use a larger can. (Old worms never die, they just worm their way into larger cans.)

● **Zymurgy's Law on the Availability of Volunteer Labor.** People are always available for work in the past tense.

● **Zymurgy's Seventh Exception to Murphy's Laws.** When it rains it pours.

(The truth can now be told. The oft-quoted Zymurgy is actually Conrad Schneiker.)

Collection/ Source Code

AIC   Advanced Instruments' "Compilation of Very Important but Little Known Scientific Principles." A brochure, numbered SNAFU 8695, put out by this Newton Highlands, Mass., company about 1970.

AO   Allan L. Otten of *The Wall Street Journal.* From his files and columns on the subject.

ASF   *Astounding Science Fiction.* From that magazine's long-running series of letters on laws. (See *Finagle File* for a fuller description.)

Co.   A notation indicating *Common*—i.e., difficult to pin to any collection because it appears in so many.

FD   Fred Dyer's collection.

FL   "Farber's Laws." From an article of that title in *The New York Times Magazine* for March 17, 1968.

HE   Hans Einstein, the RAND Corp.

HW   *Harper's* "Wraparound." Laws solicited from readers for the section of "Wraparound" items in the August, 1974, issue.

JE   John Erhman computerized collection housed at the Stanford Linear Accelerator Center.

JIR   *The Journal of Irreproducible Results.*

JMcC   John McClaughry, Concord, Vt.

JW   Jack Womeldorf, collector-in-residence, Library of Congress.

"LSP"   "Life's Simple Philosophies." A Xeroxed collection of laws that I have been unable to attribute to any person or publica-

tion. Several copies were sent to me by people who found copies circulating around their offices.

MB *Malice in Blunderland,* Thomas Martin's important book (McGraw-Hill, 1971.)

MBC Mark B. Cohen, Pennsylvania House of Representatives.

MLS Marshall L. Smith, research director, WMAL Radio, Washington, D.C. A maker and collector of laws.

POR "Principles of Operations Research." From the series of articles by Robert Machol that have appeared in *Interfaces.*

PQ *Peter's Quotations.* Dr. Lawrence J. Peter's invaluable reference.

RS Robert Specht, the RAND Corp.

Scientific Collections Designation for several one-page collections of "Scientific Laws" found floating through or tacked up in such places as the National Institutes of Health and the National Bureau of Standards.

S.T.L. The *Schneiker/Townsend/Logg et al.* collection from the University of Arizona.

TO'B Tom O'Brien, the Department of Labor.

2p? A two-page set of laws in my files that is unreferenced.

U *Unknown,* at least to the author.

Report from the Director

- **Newton's Other Law.** If I have seen further, it is by standing on the shoulders of giants.
  (Sir Isaac Newton, February 18, 1676.)

Since the creation of the Murphy Center for the Codification of Human and Organizational Law, dozens of people have come forth to offer laws of their own discovery or examples which they have collected from others. In order to properly acknowledge these people, they have been appointed to positions at the Center and are listed on the following pages.

With the help of these people more than 2,000 laws have been collected to date with still more coming in. For this reason —and because it tends to prove that the Center fills a void in American life—it will remain open indefinitely continuing to collect laws for possible enlarged editions or new collections. The address:

Paul Dickson, Director
The Murphy Center for the Codification
of Human and Organizational Law
Box 80
Garrett Park, Md. 20766

Two classes of position have been created by the Center, with the senior appointments reserved for those whose contributions have been truly major.

Senior Fellows

Nancy H. Dickson
Fred Dyer
John Ehrman
Edward Logg
Alan Otten

Conrad Schneiker
Marshall L. Smith
Robert D. Specht
Gregg Townsend
Jack Womeldorf

Fellows

Clyde F. Adams
Patricia Altobello
Joe Anderson
Don Bailey
A. J. Barton
Edmund C. Berkeley
Judith de Mille Berson
James Blankenship
Murray Teigh Bloom
Bruce O. Boston
Charlie Boyle
Ben Bova
Howard Bray
Nicholas Bretagna II
John Bright–Holmes
Larry W. Bryant
Gil Butler
Jo Cahow
Terry Catchpole
Mark B. Cohen
Ray Connolly
Robert Cook
John H. Corcoran, Jr.
Walter J. Crowell

James I. Davis
John Dean
Anne Denmark
Raj K. Dhawan
Bob Duckles
Gov. Pierre du Pont
Bob Einbinder
Hans Einstein
James T. Evans
David and Jayne Evelyn
Doug Evelyn
Richard N. Farmer
Edgar R. Fiedler
R. S. Freedman
F. Buckminster Fuller
Ray Geiger
Gents of East Russell Hall, U.
   of Georgia
David Gerrold
G. Gestra
Michael F. Goff
Vic Gold
Valerie Golvig
Joseph C. Goulden

Sherry Graditor
Daniel S. Greenberg
Douglas Guerette
Betty Hartig
Charles D. Hartman
John W. Hazard
Paul Herbig
Raymond M. Hill
Charles Issawi
Robert A. Jackson
Dr. Arthur Kasspe
M. M. "Johnny" Johnson
Dr. James Kane
Amron H. Katz
Erwin Knoll
Martin S. Kottmeyer
Martin Krakowski
Alan Ladwig
Linda A. Lawyer
Marion Levy
Jack Limpert
Bob Luke
Robert Machol
Peter Maiken
Frank Mankiewitz
Michael Marien
Thomas L. Martin
Frank Martineau
Robert E. Maston
Sharon Mathews
John McClaughry
Juliet McGhie
Gerard E. McKenna
J. R. Meditz
Donald A. Metz

Joe Miller
Michael T. Minerath
Van Mizzell, Jr.
Dr. Fitzhugh Mullan
Kent Myers
Helen Neal
Gary Novak
Tom O'Brien
Bill O'Neill
Bob Orben
Denys Parsons
John Peers
Douglas Pike
Jody Powell
Dan Rapoport
Barbara and Marcus Raskin
Phyllis Richman
Dan Roddick
Jane Ross
Mike Ross
Steve Ross
Rick Scanlon
John L. Shelton
Robert Skole
Bob Smith
Robert J. Smith
Dee Solomon
Robert Sommer
Jim Srodes
Charles Suhor
Dan Sullivan
John Thornton
Dr. Leo Troy
Marcello Truzzi
Johnathan Waddell

Michael J. Wagner
Roy W. Walters
Sam W. Warren
Jay Weisman
Rozanne Weissman
Nancy Wells
Bob Wilson

Hal John Wimberly
Gary Witzenburg
Wizard of FM 101
Donald F. Wood
William K. Wright
Will Yolen
Mark W. Zemansky

In addition the Director would like to thank the following periodicals for running the Center's appeal for laws: *Association Trends, FASST News, New Engineer, Playboy,* and *Washingtonian.*

Index

A

Abstraction: *Booker's*
Absurdity: *Boultbee's*
Academia: *Abbott's; Barzun's; Bok's; Bombeck's (Principles); Dawes-Bell; Duggan's; Father; Gummidge's; Herrnstein's; Hildebrand's; Kerr-Martin; Martin's (Laws); May's; Murphy's; Nyquist's; Ozian; Sayre's; Waffle's; Weisman's*
Accidents: *Frankel's; Titanic*
Accomplishment: *Bucy's; Evans's; Golden*
Accuracy: *Accuracy*
Acoustics: *Restaurant*
Adjournment: *Committee*
Advertising: *Advertising; Dawes-Bell; Drucker*
Advice: *Dave's (Law), Expert*
Age: *Baruch's; Lynott's; Paige's*
Aggression: *Issawi's*
Air: *Nations*
Airplanes/Air Transportation/Aviation: *Douglas's; Durrell's; Mills's (Law of Transportation Logistics); Witzenburg's*
Alcohol: *Pastorés.* See also: Drink
Alienation: *Cohen's (Laws of Politics)*
Ambiguity: *Suhor's*
Ambition: *Cohen's (Laws of Politics)*
America: *Russell's*
Analysis: *Martin's (Basic); Murphy's*
Anesthesia: *Local*
Annual Reports: *Hale's*
Antiques: *Skole's*
Appearance: *Character*
Appreciation: *Inverse*
Approval: *Approval*
Architecture: *Cheops's*
Arguments: *Cutler Webster's*
Army: *Army (Axiom); Army (Law); Tishbein's*
Arrogance: *Bustlin'; Fifth*
Arts: *Golden*
Assumptions: *Burns's; Schumpeter's; Tylk's*
Astrology: *Astrology*
Attraction: *Cohen's (Laws of Politics)*
Auditors: *O'Brien's (Principle)*
Authority: *Katz's (Other)*
Authors: *Kauffmann's*
Automobiles/Automotive: *Barrett's; Berson's; Bombeck's (Principles); Bruce-Brigg's; Caen's; Cleveland's; Eternity; Fishbein's; Hartman's; Hogg's; Johnson's (First); Road; Travel*

B

Backpacking: *Barber's*
Bad Luck: *Broken*
Baldness: *Nobel's*
Banks: *Checkbook; Ettorre's; John's (Collateral); Sutton's*
Barbers: *Expert*
Bargains: *Eve's*
Baseball: *Avery (Sayings); Berra's; Smith's (Laws)*
Bathroom Hooks: *Joyce's*
Beer: *Goulden's (Axiom); Jinny's; Long's*
Beliefs: *Bartz's*
Bicycle: *Bicycle; Bicycling*
Biochemistry: *Hersh's*
Biology: *Edington's*
Birthday Parties: *Richman's*
Books: *Atwood's; Joyce's; NASA*
Boomerangs: *Mudgeeraba*
Boredom: *Levy's*
Borrowing: *Bill Babcock's; Billings's (Law)*
Bosses: *Work*
Brains: *Ozian*
Bread and Butter: *Murphy's; Perversity (of Nature); Selective; Sod's*
Brevity: *Katz's (Other)*
Bribery: *Bribery*
Bridge: *Bridge; Orwell's*
Briefings: *Katz's (Maxims)*
Budgets: *Bolton's; Cheops's; Pratt*
Bureaucracy: *Acheson's; Boren's; Branch's; Brown's (J.); Bureaucracy; Bureaucratic Cop-Out; Bureaucratic Laws; Cohn's; Displaced; Evelyn's; Fowler's; Gammon's; Imhoff's; McNaughton's; Melcher's; Meskimen's; Miles's; Mills's (Law); Nies's; Rodovic's; Smith's (Principle)*
Buses: *Corcoroni's; Ross's (S.)*
Business: *Brown's (Law of Business Success); Davis's (Laws); Drucker; McLandress's; Pareto's; Peter Principle; Robertson's*

C

Calculators: *Murphy's; Shelton's*
Campaigns: *O'Brien's (First); Rakove's; Walinsky's*
Candidates: *Gold's (V.); Kelley's; Nobel's; Nofziger's; Prime; Public Relations; Spencer's*
Canoeing: *Andrew's*

Cant: *Thermopolitical*
Capitalism: *Bustlin'*
Cards: *Canada*
Caricature: *LePelley's*
Cats: *Long's; Short's*
Celebrity: *Avery (Sayings)*
Celibacy: *Socio-Genetics*
Chance: *Langin's*
Character: *Character*
Checkbook: *Checkbook*
Chickens: *Purina*
Children: *Crane's (Rule); Cripp's; Gumperson's (Law); Kaplan's; Old; Richman's; Schickel's*
Chili: *Chili*
Christmas: *Christmas*
CIA: *Camp's*
Circuits: *Cushman's*
Civilization: *Allen's (Law)*
Civil Service: *Nader's*
Clerks: *Drucker*
Clothing: *Eve's*
Cliches: *Short's*
Clutter: *Boston's; Dorm*
Colleges/Universities: *Bombeck's (Principles); Dawes-Bell; Dorm Room; Institutional; May's; Murphy's; Weisman's*
Comedy: *K Rule; Lindy's*
Commissions: *Connolly's (Rule)*
Committees: *Boyle's; Committee; Fiedler's; Issawi's; Kettering's; Martin's; (Laws); Oeser's*
Communications: *Martin's (Laws)*
Company/Corporation: *Hale's*
Competence/Incompetence: *Boyle's; Cornuelle's; Evelyn's; Freemon's; G Constant; Paul; Peter Principle; Riggs's*
Competition: *Cohen's (Law of Politics)*
Complaints: *Zimmerman's (Law of Complaints)*
Complexity: *Anderson's; Malek's; Martin's (Basic); Oaks's; Peter Principle*
Computer: *Brooks's; Computability; Computer; Computer Programming; Dijkstra's; Drucker; Gallois's; Gilb's; Golob's; Gray's (Law of Programming); Grosch's; IBM; Logg's; Mesmerisms; Customer's; Pareto's; Weinberg's*
Conferences: *Committee; Czecinski's; Zusmann's*
Confusion: *Everitt's; Rumsfeld's*
Constants: *G Constant; Osborn's*
Consultants: *NASA*
Consumption: *Issawi's*
Contracts: *Connolly's (Law); Goldwyn's; Katz's*
Contradictions: *Proverbial*
Control: *Riesman's*
Copiers: *Murphy's*
Corrections: *Editorial*
Corruption: *Miller's (N.)*
Cosmic Irreversibility: *Fuller's*
Costs: *Connolly's (Law); Grosch's*
Coups: *Camp's*
Courses: *Hildebrand's*
Creativity: *Fitz-Gibbon's; Idea*
Credibility: *Clopton's; Nessen's; Symington's; Whispered*
Crisis: *Branch's; Dennis's*

Crowds: *Mankiewicz's*
Culpability: *Kerr's*
Culture: *Raspberry*
Customs: *Ettorre's*
Cynic: *Issawi's*

D

Data: *Finagle*
Deans: *Father*
Death: *Eternity; Gumperson's (Proof); Montagu's; Stephens's*
Debt: *Peterson's*
Decisions/Decision making: *Cooke's; Drucker; Falkland's; Kharasch's; Murphy's; Rudin's; Wolf's*
Defeat: *White*
Delay: *Bruce-Brigg's; Chisholm's; Clyde's; De-Caprio's; Dilwether's; Ettorre's; Finagle; Jinny's; Parkinson's; Plotnick's*
Democracy: *Davidson's; Jacquin's; Putney's*
Democrat: *How To*
Dentists: *Professionals'*
Design: *Parsons's*
Development: *Index; Issawi's*
Diploma: *Ozian*
Diplomacy: *Fifth*
Discovery: *Serendipity*
Distance: *Berson's; Distance; Xerces*
Divorce: *Hartig's*
Doctors: *Professionals'*
Dogmatism: *Issawi's*
Domestic Tranquility: *Barr's*
Doubt: *Boren's*
Duality: *Dude's*

E

Ecology: *Commoner's; Ehrlich's; Hardin's (G.)*
Economics: *Baer's; Billings's (Law); Bloom's; Bolton's; Buchwald's; Butler's; Dawes-Bell; Dunn's; Economist's; Fiedler's; Gammon's; Golden; Lani's; Michehl's; Peterson's; Schenk's; Schultz's*
Editors: *Froben's; O'Brien's (Law)*
Education: *Bok's.* See also: Academic, Colleges, Teachers
Ego: *Deitz's*
Elections: *Dirksen's; Gold (V.); Kelley's; Mankiewicz's; McClaughry's (Law); Nobel's; Nofziger's; Office; Three*
Electricity/Electronics: *Cushman's; First; Froud's; Parsons's*
Elegance: *Hartig's*
Elevators: *Longfellow's; Sharkey's; Tribune*
Employment: *Dawes-Bell*
Enemies: *Geanangel's*
Engineers: *Engineer's; Panic*
Entropy: *Short's*
Environment: *Inverse; Mankiewicz's*

205

Orben's; Parsons's; Phelps's (Law of Reno-
vation); Rapoport's; Rebecca's; Ross's (A.);
Sattingler's; Yapp's
Human Condition: Abbott's; Agnes Allen's; Ap-
proval; Army (Axiom); Artz's; Avery's (Ob-
servation); Baker's; Baruch's; Beauregard's;
Benchley's; Bennett's; Boozer's; Borkow-
ski's; Broken; Butler's; Chamberlain's;
Character; Chatauqua; Checkbook; Chi-
sholm; Clark's (Law); Cohen's (Choice);
Cohn's; Colson's; Dibble's; Ehrman's;
Eliot's; Farber's; Fetridge's; Franklin's (Law);
Glasow's; Goodfader's; Hardin's (G.);
Howe's; How To; John's (Axiom); Jones's;
Kafka's; Kettering's; Kirkup's; Koppett's;
Kristol's; Langin's; LaRochefoucauld's;
Leahy's; Ledge's; Levy's; Lewis's; Liebling's;
Lowrey's; Luce's; Man's; Marshall's (Uni-
versal); McGurk's; Mencken's (Law);
Mencken's (Metalaw); Miller's (M.);
Miller's (?); Munnecke's; Murphy's; Mur-
stein's; Navy; Newton's; Nixon's; North;
No. 3; O'Brien's (Rule); Occam's; O'-
Toole's; Paige's; Paradox; Pardo's; Pas-
tore's; Paturi; Peer's; Pierson's; Potter's;
Probable; Professor; Pudder's; Robertson's;
Rowe's; Rudin's; Runyon's; Sattler's;
Schuckit's; Scriptural; Segal's; Simon's; Sin-
ner's; Sprague's; Sturgeon's; Third; Tho-
reau's (Law); Thoreau's (Rule); Uhlmann's;
Unnamed; Unspeakable; Walker's; Weid-
ner's; Weiler's; Wicker's; Wilcox's; Wolf's;
Woman's; Work; Yapp's; Zymurgy's (First);
Zymurgy's (Seventh)
Human Interaction: Chisholm
Human Rights: Human
Humility: Bustlin'
Hypotheses: Edington's

I

Iceberg: Marshall's (Generalized)
Ideas: Boyle's; Fried's; Harden (F.); Idea; Katz's
(Maxims); Kettering's; Malek's; Truths
Ignorance: Short's
Inconvenience: Koppett's
Inertia: Inertia
Infernal Dynamics: Gerrold's
Influence: Greenberg's
Information: Boyle's; Cooke's; Finagle; Gray's
(Law of Bilateral Asymmetry); Kennedy's;
Mesmerisms; Ubell's
Inlaws: Clark's (First Law of Relativity)
Insanity: Kriedt's
Insertion: Fudd's (Law)
Inside Dope: Cohen's (Laws of Politics)
Institutions: Kharasch's
Insurance: Friendship
Intervention: Schuckit's
Invention/Innovation: Katz's (Maxims); Saun-
der's; Terman's

J

Jackpot: Flip
Jobs: Becker's; Cornuelle's; Dawes-Bell;
McGovern's; Wing-Walker
Journals: O'Brien's (Law); Parkinson's
Junk: Boston's; Farmer's; Hogg's; Lloyd-Jones's;
Orben's
Jury: Goulden's (Law)
Justice: Alley's; Goulden's (Law)

K

Keys: Key

L

Labor: Labor
Language: Beardsley's; K Rule
Late-Comers: Late-Comers
Law/Lawyers: Alley's; Beardsley's; Goulden's
(Law); Lawyer's (Rule); Oaks's; Parliament;
Professionals; Specht's
Lawmaking/Legislation: Cohen's (Laws of Poli-
tics); du Pont's; Finagle; Funkhouser's; Jac-
quin's; Knowles's; Mencken's (Law); Parlia-
ment
Laws: Faber's; Short's
Laziness: Saunder's
Leadership: Boyle's; Jaroslovsky's; Matsch's
Learning: Barzun; Donsen's
Liberals: Kerr-Martin; Levy's; Mankiewicz's;
McClaughry's (Second); Price's (Law of
Politics)
Life: Kerr's (General); Paige's; Rumsfeld's
Light Bulbs: Occam's
Lincoln: Lincoln
Lines: Ettorre's; Sam's
Loans: John's (Collateral)
Lobbying: du Pont's; Will's
Long-Range: Long-Range
Lost Objects: Boob's
Luggage: Hogg's
Lunch: Kelly's

M

Machines: IBM; Rural
Male: Algren's; Beifeld's; Mother
Management: Boyle's; Brien's; Brontosaurus;
Brown's (Law of Business Success); Bureau-
cratic Laws; Dennis's; Dror's (First);
Drucker; Hacker's (Law of Personnel);
Heller's; Jay's; Johnson's (Corollary); Mes-
merisms; Truths; Walters's; Wolf's

Manure: *OHSA's*
Maps: *Parsons's*
Marketing: *Drucker; Lewis's*
Marriage: *O'Neill's*
Mate: *Instant*
Math: *Ashley-Perry*
Measurement: *Coomb's; Finagle; Schultze's; Westheimer's*
Media: *Bagdikian's; Blanchard's; Considine's; Deitz's; du Pont's; Editorial; Foster's; Funkhouser's; Germond's; Gold (V.); Gold (W.); Hagerty's; Kauffmann's; Kent's; Knoll's; Loevinger's; Marcus's; Nessen's; O'Brien's (Principle); O'Doyle's; O'Neill's; Pike's; Rather's; Rumsfeld's; Ubell's; Weaver's; Wilson's (W.)*
Medicare/Medicaid: *Drucker*
Medicine: *Bombeck's (Rule); Davis's (Basic); Drucker; Local; Parkinson; Professionals'; Roemer's*
Meetings: *Czecinski's; Kirkland's; Late-Comers; McLaughlin's; Parson's; Shanahan's; Wolf's*
Memory: *Grobe's*
Memos: *Acheson's; Boyle's; Corcoran's*
Menus: *Calkins's*
Military: *Vance's; White*
Mineral Rights: *Getty's*
Mirrors: *Broken*
Misery: *Baker's; How To*
Mishap: *Chisholm*
Misunderstanding: *Chisholm*
Model Railroading: *Bye's*
Monday: *Avery (Sayings)*
Money: *Billings's (Law); Bolton's; Butler's; Canada; DeCaprio's; Donohue's; Dunn's; Evelyn's; Golden; Gresham's; Gross's; Gumperson's (Law); Instant; John's (Collateral); Lani's; Long's; Miller's (J.); Money; Murchison's; Pardo's; Pratt; Raskin's; Sam's; Sutton's; Truth's; Vance's*
Mortgage: *Journalist's*
Motivation: *Drucker*
Movies: *Shalit's*

N

Names: *Cohen's (J.); Curley's*
Nations: *Hacker's (Law); Index; Issawi's; Miller's (N.); Moynihan's; Nations*
Natural Law: *Long's; Murphy's*
Nature: *Darwin's; Fetridge's; Gumperson's (Law); Harvard; Long's; Murphy's; Perversity (of Nature); Short's*
Necessity: *Farber's*
Neighbors: *Issawi's*
Newspapers: See: Press
New York Times: Nobel
Nobel: *Nobel*
Non-Smokers: *Dhawan's*

O

Obituaries: *Blanchard's*
Objects (Perversity of): *Bernstein's; Boob's; Boyle's; Chatauqua; Chisholm; Cushman's; Ear's; Finagle; Flap's; Fudd's (First); Gerrold's; Murphy's; Perversity (of Nature); Perversity (of Production); Rapoport's; Ross's (A.); Sattler's; Selective; Universal; Waddell's*
Offensiveness: *Brown's (S.)*
Office Holders: *Office Holder's*
Oil: *Dirksen's (Version); Issawi's; Sadat's*
Opposition: *Fudd's (First); Galbraith's (Law of Prominence)*
Optimist/Optimism: *Oppenheimer's; O'Toole's; Wolf's*
Orders: *Army (Axiom)*
Organization: *Boyle's; Brien's; Brontosaurus; Dow's; Drucker; Evelyn's; Gadarene; G Constant; Golub's; Gray's (Law of Bilateral Asymmetry); Hacker's (Law); Hacker's (Law of Personnel); How To; Imhoff's; Johnson's (Corollary); Katz's (Maxims); Kharasch's; Miles's; Navy; No. 3; Oeser's; Parkinson's; Rodovic's; Vail's; Zimmerman's*
Oz: *Ozian*

207

P

Packaging: *Orben's*
Pain: *Science*
Paperwork: *Brown's (J.); Brown's (Law of Business Success); Corcoran's; Dyer's; Fowler's; Katz's (Maxims); Mesmerisms; Oeser's; Von Braun's*
Parades: *Wells's*
Paranoia: *How To; Pastore's*
Parking: *Jaroslavsky's; Joyce's; Murphy's*
Parliamentary Procedure: *Swipple*
Parties: *Ear's*
Pencils: *Avery (Sayings); Murphy's; No. 3; Price's (Law of Science)*
Perfection: *Stephens's*
Permanence: *Cohen's (Law of Politics)*
Personnel: *Hacker's (Law of Personnel)*
Pessimist/Pessimism: *Oppenheimer's; O'Toole's; Wolf's*
Ph.Ds: *Duggan's*
Philosophy: *Gardener's; Harris's (Law)*
Pills: *Davis's (Basic)*
Pipe: *Pipe*
Pizza: *Kerr's (Three)*
Planning: *Wolf's*
Plants: *Bombeck's (Rule)*
Plumbing: *Gardner's; Phelps's (Law of Renovation)*
Poetry: *Ciardi's*
Policy: *Dror's (First); Dror's (Second); Wilson's (J.Q.)*

Political Incumbent: *Connolly's (Rule)*
Politics: *Acton's; Baer's; Boultbee's; Broder's; Cohen's (Laws of Politics); Connolly's (Rule); Curley's; Dirksen's (Three); Evans's (Law of Political Perfidy); Galbraith's (Law of Political Wisdom); Gilmer's; Gold's (V.); Halberstam's; How To; Jacquin's; John Adams's; Johnson's (Prior); Kamin's; Mankiewicz's; McCarthy's; McClaughry's (Law); Munncke's; Nobel's; Nofziger's; O'Brien's (First); Office; Politician's; Powell's (A.C.); Price's (Law of Politics); Public Relations; Rakove's; Randolph's; Rayburn's; Rumsfeld's; Sayre's; Shaffer's; Smith's (Laws); Spencer's; Symington's; Thermopolitics; Truman's; Wallinsky's; Will's*
Postage Stamp: *How To*
Poverty: *Davis's (Laws)*
Power: *Acton's; Bonafede's; Dirksen's (Version); Drucker; Evans's (Law of Political Perfidy); Grandma; Hein's; John Adams's; Oeser's*
Practical Advice: *Allen's (Axiom); Allen's (Distinction); Baldy's; Bartz's; Beauregard's; Benchley's; Berkeley's; Berra's; Bill Babcock's; Bloom's Boozer's; Dave's (Law); Dave's (Rule); Hartley's; How To; Hull's; Rebecca's; Sattlinger's; Suhor's*
Practicality: *Cohen's (Laws of Politics)*
Pregnancy: *Bombeck's (Principles)*
Presidents: *Broder's; Coolidge's; Johnson's (Prior); Lincoln; McLandress's; Nixon's; Nobel's; Rumsfeld's; Truman's*
Press: *Bagdikian's; Blanchard's; Considine's; Deitz's; du Pont's; Editorial; Foster's; Funkhouser's; Germond's; Gold (V.); Gold (W.); Gray's (Law of Bilateral Asymmetry); Greener's; Gresham's; Crump's; Hagerty's; Journalist's; Kauffmann's; Kent's; Knoll's; Loevinger's; Marcus's; Moynihan's; Nessen's; Nobel; O'Brien's (Principle); O'Doyle's; O'Neill's; Otten's (Law of Typesetting); Pike's; Powell's (J.); Rather's; Rumsfeld's; Weaver's; Wilson's (W.); Yolen's; Zellar's*
Press Secretary (Presidential): *Nessen's; Powell's (J.); Ross's (C.); Salinger's*
Price: *Graditor's*
Principle: *Evans's; Shaffer's*
Probabilities: *Fourth; Gumperson's (Law)*
Problem-Solving: *Abrams's; Accuracy; Allen's (Axiom); Anderson's; Berkeley's; Billings's (Phenomenon); Booker's; Boob's; Boren's; Boyle's; Bucy's; Bureaucracy; Bureaucratic Laws; Burns; Cliff-Hanger; Cooke's; Crane's (Rule); Dijkstra's; Displaced; Dobbin's; Dror's (First); Epstein's; Evvie Nef's; Murphy's; Optimum; Peers's; Pratt; Rowe's; Rural; Sattingler's; Sevareid's; Shelton's; Short's; Skinner's; Wolf's; Zymurgy's (First)*
Procedures: *Chisholm*
Procrastination: *Inertia*
Production/Productivity: *Gammon's; Luten's; Perversity (of Production); Rogers's; Scientific*
Products: *Boyle's*

Professors: *Lenin's*
Profits: *Hale's*
Programming: *Brooks's; Computer Programming; Dijkstra's; Gilb's; Gray's (Law of Programming); Halpern's; Hoare's; Logg's; Weinberg's*
Progress: *Bustlin'; Butler's; Issawi's; Nienberg's*
Projects: *Bureaucratic Laws; Serendipity*
Prominence: *Galbraith's (Law of Prominence)*
Prototype: *Bye's*
Proverbs: *Proverbial*
Psychology: *Maier's*
Public: *Gummidge's*
Public Opinion: *Politician's*
Public Relations: *Public Relations (Client); Public Relations (Prime Rule); Rogers's; Ross's (C.); Salinger's; Ubell's*
Public Service: *Branch's*
Public Speaking: *Public Speaking*
Public Works: *Cleveland's*
Publishing: *Froben's; Murphy's*

Q

Quality: *Herblock's; Perversity (of Production)*

R

Racial Integration: *Simmon's*
Raffles: *Gumperson's (Law)*
Reality: *Sprague's*
Reform: *Reform*
Reliability: *Gilb's*
Religion: *Vique's*
Renovation: *Phelps's (Law of Renovation)*
Repairmen: *Schenk's*
Reports: *Cohn's; Mesmerisms*
Republicans: *How To*
Research and Development (R&D): *Extended; Gordon's; Lubin's; Murstein's; NASA; Parkinson's; Patrick's; Phases; Price's (Law of Science); Scientific; Wilson's (J.Q.)*
Resignation: *Galbraith's (Law of Political Wisdom)*
Restaurants: *Algren's; Calkins's; Chinese; Germond's; Harris's (Restaurant); Restaurant; Tipper's*
Results: *Riddle's*
Retirement: *Mosher's*
Revenge: *Dirksen's (Three)*
Rhetoric: *Dunne's*
Right: *McKenna's*
Risk: *Katz's (Maxims)*
Roller Skates: *Rapoport's*
Romance: *Jacoby's*
Routine: *Evelyn's*
Routing Slips: *Melcher's*
Rules: *Boquist's; Ginsberg's; Golden; Thoreau's (Rules)*
Rural: *Rural*

S

Salaries: *Mesmerisms; Riesman's*
Salesmen: *Drucker; Schenk's*
Sample: *Sells's*
Sanity: *Kreidt's*
Schedules: *Cheops's; Corcoroni's; Finagle; Ninety; Ross's* (S.)
Schemes: *Howe's*
Schools: *Boozer's; Mankiewicz's; Murphy's*
Science and Technology: *Allen's (Axiom); Ashley-Perry; Asimov's; Berkeley's; Billings's (Phenomenon); Blaaw's; Booker's; Bowie's; Boyle's; Bustlin'; Carson's; Chisholm's; Clarke's; Compensation; Computability; Coomb's; Edington's; Extended; Finagle; First; Fudge; Futility; Gall's; Golden; Gordon's; Harvard; Katz's (Other); Kohn's; Levian's; Lowrey's; Lubin's; Maier's; NASA; Nobel; O'Brien's (Law); Parkinson's; Patrick's; Phases; Pratt; Price's (Law of Science); Purina; Riddle's; Sattingler's; Schumpeter's; Science; Scientific; Technology; Woodward's*
Scriptural: *Scriptural*
Second-Ratedness: *Second-Ratedness*
Secrecy: *Cohen's (Law of Politics); Long's*
Security: *Security; Wing-Walker; Wober's*
Self-Importance: *Fifth*
Serendipity: *Serendipity*
Sex: *Algren's; Beifeld's; Bonafede's; Fischer's; John Cameron's*
Show Business: *Hartley's*
Side-Effects: *Commoner's; Hardin's* (G.)
Simplicity: *Occam's*
Sin: *Emerson's*
Slides: *Slide Presentation*
Smoking: *Dhawan's; Pipe*
Soap Operas: *Davis's (Laws)*
Social Class: *Hall's*
Social Engineering: *Robertson's*
Social Sciences: *Computability; Dawes-Bell; Finagle; Issawi's; Murstein's*
Society: *Everitt's; Gardner's; Instant; Technology; Thermopolitical*
Sociology: *Dibble's; Hart's*
Sound: *Culshaw's*
Space: *Hersh's*
Spaghetti: *Morley's*
Spare Parts: *Spare Parts*
Specialists: *Donsen's; Freemon's*
Speeches: *Bagdikian's*
Sports: *Ade's; Andrew's; Avery (Sayings); Barber's; Berra's; Bicycle; Bicycling; Frisbee; McCarthy's; Metz's; Mudgeeraba; Runyon's; Smith's (Laws); Terman's; Yolen's*
Station Wagons: *Hogg's*
Statistics: *Ashley-Perry; NASA; Perelman's; Stamp's*
Stocks and Bonds: *Crane's (Law); Stock Market; Stockbroker's*
Stress: *LeChatellier's*
Style: *Brown* (S.)
Subways: *Meditz*

Success: *Boyle's; Brien's; Brown's (Law of Business Success); Einstein's; Fourth; Heller's; Hollywood's; Instant; Paturi; Pike's; Sod's*
Supermarket: *Bombeck's (Principles); Ettorre's*
Supply and Demand: *Sadat's*
Support: *Evelyn's*
Surveys: *Fiedler's; Perelman's*
Survival: *Halberstam's*
System (The): *Goodfader's*
Systems: *Gall's; Gilb's; Martin's (Basic); Shaw's; Waldo's*

T

Talent: *Boyle's*
Taxes: *Diogenes's (First and Second); Eternity; Gumperson's (Proof); Lani's*
Taxis: *O'Doyle's; Taxi; Weaver's*
Tchaikovsky: *Short's*
Teachers and Teaching: *Boozer's; Herrnstein's; Kerr-Martin; Lenin's; Martin's (Laws); Waffle's*
Telephone: *Lawyer's (Law); Parkinson's*
Television: *Avery (Sayings); Boultbee's; Gresham's; Kitman's; Lindy's; Pastore's; Schickel's; Sahlit's*
Temper: *Hagerty's*
Testimony: *Otten's (Law of Testimony)*
Theories: *Berkeley's; Fiedler's; Finagle; Woodward's*
Thinking: *IBM*
Time: *Belle's; Character; Cohn's; DeCaprio's; Dunn's; Engineer's; Extended; Golub's; Hersh's; McLaughlin's; Meskimen's; Nienberg's; Ninety; O'Neill's; Otten's (Law of Testimony); Paul; Professionals'; Segal's*
Time (Magazine): *Galbraith's (Law of Prominence)*
Tinkering: *Ehrlich's*
Tips: *Tipper's*
Tires: *Fishbein's*
Titles: *McGovern's*
Toll-Booth: *Ettorre's*
Tomfoolery: *Gallois's*
Tools: *Anthony's (Law of Force); Anthony's (Law of the Workshop); Dobbins's; Gardening; Jake's; Johnson's (First); Kaplan's; Plotnick's; Spare*
Towns: *Steinbeck's*
Toys: *Christmas*
Traffic: *Bruce-Brigg's; Cleveland's; Road*
Trains: *Ross's* (S.)
Transistors: *Froud's*
Transportation / Travel: *Airplane; Corcoroni's; Durrell's; Ear's; Finagle; Hogg's; Meditz; Mills's (Law of Transportation Logistics); Ross's (S.); Sprague's; Travel; Witzenberg's*
Trash: *Orben's*
Truth: *Avery (Sayings); Clopton's; Comin's; Marshall's (Universal); Short's*
Typesetting: *Otten's (Law of Typesetting)*

U

Ultimate Laws: *Ultimate (Law); Ultimate (Principle)*
Umbrellas: *Umbrella*
Unanimity: *Levy's*
Uncertainty: *Gall's*
Understanding: *Hacker's (Law)*
Unexpected: *Peter Principle*
United: *United*
United States: *Hart's*
Universe: *Haldane's*
Urban Planning: *Wood's*

V

Vacation: *Luten's*
Vagueness: *Committee*
Variables: *Osborn's*
Vices: *Paige's*
Volunteers: *Zymurgy's (Law)*
Voters: *Connolly's (Rule)*

W

Wage and Price Controls: *Connally's*
Waking: *Long's*

War: *Bustlin'; White*
War of 1812: *Short's*
Warranty: *Graditor's*
Washington: *Dean's; Rumsfeld's*
Watches: *Segal's*
Water: *Nations*
Watergate: *Colson's; Dean's; Galbraith's (Law of Political Wisdom); Nixon's*
Wealth: *Cohen's (Law of Politics)*
Weight-Watchers: *Weight-Watcher's*
White House: *Rumsfeld's*
Wickedness: *Levy's*
Winning: *Ade's; Chamberlain's; Ginsberg's; Merrill's*
Wisdom: *Cohen's (Law of Politics); Long's; Lynott's*
Women: *Human; Jacoby's; Nyquist's; Woman's*
Words: *Smith's (Principles)*
Work: *Becker's; Belle's; Boyle's; Coolidge's; Crane's (Rule); Einstein's; Extended; Gammon's; Katz's (Maxims); Labor; Miles's; Ninety; Pastore's; Peter Principle; Phases; Pierson's; Rodovic's; Rudin's; Sam's; Spare; Third; Tom Sawyer's; Vail's; Westheimer's; Woman's; Work*
Writing: *Considine's; Davis's (Law); Faber's*
Wrong: *McKenna's*

Z

Zoning: *McClaughry's (Iron)*

Paul Dickson is a thirty-nine-year-old writer living in Garrett Park, Maryland, who became interested in the phenomenon of universal laws some years ago when he discovered that the size of the cut he inflicted upon himself while shaving was directly proportional to the importance of the event he was shaving for. This is his ninth book.